VEGETABLES

VEGETABLES

FROM THE EARTH TO THE TABLE

This edition published in 2012
LOVE FOOD is an imprint of Parragon Books Ltd

Parragon
Queen Street House
4 Queen Street
Bath BA1 1HE, UK

ISBN: 978-1-4454-8912-4

Printed in China

Introduction by Christine McFadden

Notes for the Reader
This book uses both metric and imperial measurements. Follow the same units of measurement throughout;
do not mix metric and imperial. All spoon measurements are level: teaspoons are assumed to be 5 ml, and
tablespoons are assumed to be 15 ml. Unless otherwise stated, milk is assumed to be full fat, eggs and
individual vegetables are medium, and pepper is freshly ground black pepper. Unless otherwise stated, all root
vegetables should be washed and peeled prior to using.

Garnishes, decorations and serving suggestions are all optional and not necessarily included in the recipe
ingredients or method.

The times given are an approximate guide only. Preparation times differ according to the techniques used
by different people and the cooking times may also vary from those given. Optional ingredients, variations or
serving suggestions have not been included in the time calculations.

Recipes using raw or very lightly cooked eggs should be avoided by infants, the elderly, pregnant women,
convalescents and anyone suffering from an illness. Pregnant and breastfeeding women are advised to avoid
eating peanuts and peanut products. Sufferers from nut allergies should be aware that some of the ready-
made ingredients used in the recipes in this book may contain nuts. Always check the packaging before use.

Picture acknowledgements
The publisher would like to thank Getty Images for permission to reproduce copyright material on the
following pages: 2, 5 (all), 10, 12, 15, 16–17, 18, 19 (all), 21, 24–25, 34–35, 70–71, 108–109, 144–145, 182–183

Contents

Introduction

The last few years have seen a significant change in our attitude to vegetables. Thanks to modern cultivation techniques and a renewed interest in home-grown and heritage varieties, they have become the superstars of the kitchen.

This book shows you how to make the most of this cornucopia, explaining the nutritional benefits, purchasing options, what to look for in terms of freshness, and how best to store vegetables once you get them home. Also included are the benefits of seasonal eating accompanied by lists of what is in season and when. Vegetables are grouped according to botanical characteristics, and each of the five chapters begins with a directory describing them in detail.

The Benefits of Eating Vegetables

Vegetables come in a dazzling array of shapes, sizes and flamboyant colours. They are also tasty, nutritious and fun to cook, and if you grow your own they are even more satisfying.

Now that a strong link between a diet high in vegetables and good health has been firmly established, there is almost universal agreement among government advisers that we should eat at least five portions of vegetables and fruit a day.

There is good reason to follow this advice. Vegetables are nutritional super-foods. Not only do they provide vitamins, minerals and fibre, they are also packed with other therapeutic substances that scientists believe may help protect against chronic and life-threatening diseases, such as heart disease and cancer. Among the most important substances are antioxidants, a group that includes several minerals, vitamins C and E, and carotenoids – a pigment found mainly in orange- and red-fleshed vegetables but also in dark green leafy ones. Antioxidants protect the body by deactivating harmful free radicals that attack the nucleus of body cells, causing genetic changes that have been linked to cancer.

Leafy greens, such as kale, spring greens and broccoli, are top of the league, along with red peppers, carrots and orange-fleshed squash. They are all rich sources of carotenoids and vitamin C. Avocados are also rich in vitamin C, as well as vitamin E, and are said to improve the condition of the skin and hair.

Brussels sprouts, asparagus and broccoli contain high levels of folate, one of the B vitamins needed for healthy red blood cells. The onion family is a major source of sulphur compounds, which may help suppress malignant tumours. Garlic is particularly rich in allicin, a substance said to reduce health-threatening cholesterol levels.

Pulses, such as dried beans, peas and lentils, are an excellent source of low-fat protein as well as complex carbohydrates, vitamins, minerals and fibre.

Vegetables also provide vital minerals especially needed by women: calcium to maintain bone mass later in life, and iron to help prevent anaemia. Spinach, spring greens and watercress are particularly high in calcium and contain plenty of iron. Broccoli and green peppers are also a good source of iron. Unfortunately, the iron in plants is thought to be less well absorbed than iron from animal sources, although vitamin C will help the body absorb it.

It's worth remembering that vitamins C and B complex are partially destroyed by exposure to the air, light and heat, and they also leach into the cooking water. For maximum nutritional benefit, store vegetables in a cool dark place, chop or peel them only when you are ready to use them, and eat them raw or lightly cooked. Steaming or stir-frying are the best options.

Types of Vegetables

Vegetables consist of a surprising number of different parts – shoots and stems, roots and tubers, buds, leaves, flowers and seeds – all of which we eat depending on the variety. There are also fruits, such as tomatoes and avocadoes, that are not strictly vegetables but are usually thought of as such.

Mushrooms are important plant foods too, although these are technically fungi rather than vegetables. It is this immense botanical variation that makes vegetables such an interesting part of our diet and an inspiration for the cook.

This book is split into the following five chapters with vegetables grouped according to their botanical characteristics.

Vegetable fruits

The first chapter focuses on well-known fruits, such as avocados, and Mediterranean-style produce, such as tomatoes, peppers, chillies and aubergines. These colourful vegetable fruits form the backbone of an enormous number of tasty and nutritious dishes.

The chapter also includes summer and winter squash, and pumpkins. Summer squash – courgettes and marrows, for example – have thin edible skin and are eaten whole, seeds and all, while still young and tender. Winter squash, such as butternut, are hollow with tough inedible skin. Pumpkins are similar to winter squash but they are invariably round with a flat base and orange skin.

Shoots, stems, roots and tubers

The chapter includes ground-hugging shoots and stems – asparagus, fennel and celery for instance – as well as the more common roots, such as beetroot, celeriac, carrots and radishes. Tubers are a fleshy protuberance attached to an underground sideways-growing stem. They include potatoes, sweet potatoes and Jerusalem artichokes.

Brassicas and salad leaves

Vital to health, the all-important brassica family includes leafy greens, such as spinach, kale and cabbage, as well as the less familiar chard and oriental pak choi. Brussels sprouts, which are technically leaf buds, are also part of the group, along with broccoli and cauliflower.

Salad leaves are included, too, since some of them are brassicas. They offer a wonderful variety of colours, textures and flavours, ranging from slightly bitter endive, Belgian chicory and radicchio, to peppery rocket and watercress, mild-tasting lettuce, and juicy oriental leaves, such as mizuna.

Mushrooms and the onion family

Growing from a network of underground spores, mushrooms come in an array of shapes and sizes, from the trumpet-shaped orange chanterelle to the more sombre flat-capped field mushroom. Cultivated varieties include tiny brown creminis, closed-cup chestnut mushrooms, enormous portabellos, and oriental types, such as oyster and shiitake.

The onion family includes leeks, garlic, shallots and numerous types of onion. Leeks and spring onions are upward-growing stems covered with tightly packed, fleshy leaves and moist, pliable skin. Garlic, shallots and regular onions are swollen bulbs, either single- or multi-cloved, covered with a papery dry skin. Garlic may be harvested early while the skin is still soft and silky, and the cloves are barely formed. At this stage it is known as 'wet' or 'green' garlic.

Pods and seeds

The final chapter focuses on one of the most important vegetable groups: the seeds of pod-bearing vegetables. These include peas and beans, both fresh and dried, as well as dried lentils and chickpeas. Fresh beans include green beans with edible fleshy pods, and those that need the pod removing before cooking – broad beans or fresh borlotti beans, for example.

The chapter also includes sweetcorn and beansprouts. Though botanically classified as fruit, sweetcorn is in fact another type of seed. The ears contain the kernels, which, in turn, contain the immature seeds of corn (maize). Beansprouts are the power-packed shoots that emerge from the newly germinated embryo of mung beans.

Buying Vegetables

Nowadays, supermarkets provide us with the widest choice of vegetables, usually with year-round availability. Much of the produce is pre-packaged, pre-washed and pre-prepared – a great convenience for those leading action-packed lives.

For freshness and seasonality, however, it's hard to beat a good farm shop. The best grow their own vegetables and harvest them on a daily basis. The produce is not necessarily cheap, but it is generally of very good quality. Farmers' markets are another option. The vegetables on sale are locally grown i.e. within the county itself or within a defined radius, and the grower is likely to be there to tell you about them.

An alternative for those with little time to visit farm shops is the vegetable box scheme. A box of vegetables is delivered to your door on a regular basis. You do not necessarily know what will be in the box, but it will be a selection of whatever happens to be in season. You may need to find inspiring ways of cooking the same vegetable; some box schemes provide recipes to help with this.

Organic vegetables

Organic vegetables are undeniably expensive – they are grown on a smaller scale than conventional produce, and production and transportation costs are therefore higher. Even so, many people prefer organic vegetables on the grounds that they have not been dowsed with artificial fertilizers and pesticides, nor have they been genetically modified. Increasing awareness of the connection between health and diet has also fuelled demand.

Though there is a lack of conclusive evidence that organic vegetables are better for you, it's hard to deny that they are often tastier than conventionally grown produce. That said, it is important to bear in mind that this may well be due to the skill of the grower, or the particular vegetable variety, or simply because the vegetables have been grown locally, picked at the peak of ripeness and sold immediately.

Growing your own

There are few greater pleasures than growing your own vegetables, harvesting them as and when you need to, and knowing that what you are eating is absolutely fresh. You also get to try varieties that aren't normally available in the shops.

Even if space is limited, a surprising number of vegetables can be grown in pots and window boxes. Easiest and reliable croppers for the beginner are radishes, cherry tomatoes, peas and green beans. Potatoes can be grown in a special deep potato bag, available from seed merchants and garden centres.

Salad leaves are also rewarding crops – try rocket, land cress and some of the more colourful lettuces that are rarely seen in the shops. Herbs, such as chives, parsley and thyme, are invaluable in the kitchen and easy to grow in pots.

Checking for freshness

There is no knowing how long loose vegetables will remain fresh once you get them home. Pre-packed vegetables will usually be marked with a 'display until' date, but that is still no guarantee that they will last until then. Buying well within the date will help, as does knowing what to look for in terms of appearance.

Vegetable fruits

Aubergines: Look for firm-textured fruits with glossy, smooth skin. Avoid any with brown patches.

Avocados: Look for fruits that give slightly when pressed – a sign that they are ready to eat. Hard ones will ripen at room temperature within a few days.

Chillies and peppers: Look for firm fruits with smooth skin. Avoid any with soft patches.

Courgettes: Look for firm fruits that feel heavy for their size. Avoid any with broken skin.

Cucumbers: Look for firm, stiff fruits that do not feel spongy or flabby.

Pumpkins and winter squash: Look for fruits that feel heavy for their size. Avoid any with soft spots or damaged skin.

Tomatoes: Look for firm fruits with smooth skin, preferably with the green calyx attached.

Shoots

Asparagus: Look for crisp spears with tightly closed tips. Avoid any with wrinkled stems or slimy tips.

Globe artichoke: Look for heads with stiff, tightly packed leaves.

Stems

Celery: Look for heads with crisp stalks. Avoid any with brown patches.

Fennel: Look for tightly packed bulbs, preferably with a few green fronds attached. Avoid any with brown patches.

Roots

Beetroot: Look for firm, round bulbs with leaves attached.

Carrots: Look for firm, brightly coloured roots with fresh green leaves, if attached. Avoid any with sprouting yellow rootlets, cracks, small holes, or soft brown bruises.

Celeriac: Look for firm bulbs that feel heavy for their size. Avoid any with soft spots or rotting roots.

Radishes: Look for small- to medium-sized bulbs, preferably with roots and leaves attached. Avoid any that feel spongy when pinched.

Tubers

Jerusalem artichokes: Look for firm, undamaged tubers. Avoid any that are bruised or broken.

Potatoes: Look for firm, undamaged tubers. Avoid any that are sprouting or have green patches.

Sweet potatoes: Look for firm small- to medium-sized tubers.

Brassicas

Broccoli: Look for bright green heads. Avoid any that are flabby, yellowing or cracked at the cut end of the stalk.

Brussels sprouts: Look for firm, tightly packed buds. Avoid any with yellow leaves.

Cabbage: Look for heads that feel heavy for their size, with crisp leaves. Avoid any with yellowing outer leaves, and those that have been stripped.

Cauliflower: Look for cream-coloured, tightly packed heads with crisp outer leaves.

Chard, kale and pak choi: Look for crisp, fresh leaves and firm stalks. Avoid any that are limp or yellowing, or have bruised stalks.

Spinach: Look for dewy-fresh, dark green leaves. Avoid any that are bruised, yellowing or slimy.

Salad leaves

Chicory: Look for firm, elongated heads. Avoid any with green tips or slimy brown marks along the leaf edges.

Lettuce and endive: Look for dewy-fresh leaves and firm hearts.

Radicchio: Look for firm, tightly-packed heads. Avoid any that have had the outer leaves removed.

Rocket, watercress and miscellaneous small leaves: Look for fresh, bright green leaves. Avoid any that are yellowing or slimy.

Mushrooms

Cultivated and wild mushrooms: Look for clean, slightly damp caps that smell fresh. Avoid any that look dry or are slimy.

Onion family

Garlic, onions and shallots: Look for plump, solid bulbs with tight skin.

Leeks: Look for small- to medium-sized firm, white shafts. Avoid any with heavily trimmed or yellowing tops.

Spring onions: Look for firm, stiff stems with bright green tips. Avoid any that look dry or slimy.

Pods and seeds

Beansprouts: Look for fresh-looking shoots. Avoid any that are brown or slimy.

Broad beans: Look for small- to medium-sized pods. Avoid any with large bumps.

Green beans: Look for crisp pods with a satiny sheen. Avoid runner beans that are excessively fibrous or very long.

Peas: Look for crisp, green pods. Avoid any that are yellowing or fibrous.

Sweetcorn: Look for moist silks and husks, and soft, plump kernels. Husks should completely enclose the kernels.

Frozen vegetables

There is clear evidence that the longer fresh vegetables are stored, the more their valuable nutrients degrade. Since freezing usually takes place very shortly after harvesting, when nutrients are at their peak, shop-bought frozen vegetables are often a better bet than fresh ones that are out of season. Home-frozen vegetables are equally nutritious as long as they are in top condition at the time of freezing.

Most frozen vegetables can be stored for 9–12 months at -18°C/0°F or below, though there will be some loss of quality as the months go by. Do not refreeze vegetables once thawed, as the texture will suffer.

Canned vegetables

Canned vegetables are an acceptable nutritional alternative to fresh or frozen vegetables, though there will be some loss of nutrients and texture because of the heat treatment involved in the canning process.

Particularly useful are tomatoes, beans, chickpeas and lentils.

Look for cans labelled 'no salt or sugar added'. Rinse well before use and do not over-cook when reheating. Always check the 'use-by' date and throw out any cans that are rusty, dented or swollen.

Dried vegetables

Some vegetables, such as tomatoes, can be purchased in dried form. These may need to be soaked in warm water for 20–30 minutes before use or may be packed in oil. Pulses are also sold dried, making them useful ingredients to have in your store cupboard. They are cheaper than canned pulses, but they do need to be soaked overnight and then boiled from anything from 30 minutes to 2 hours, depending on the type and age of the pulse.

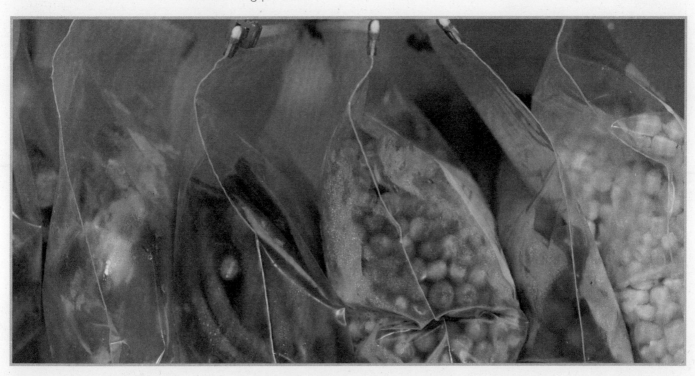

Seasonal Eating

Rightly or wrongly, today's global market place means we are no longer limited to vegetables that are in season. We can buy vegetables grown virtually anywhere in the world all year round, although often at the expense of flavour. Nowadays, however, many of us are opting to eat vegetables only when they are in season and, more often than not, only those grown locally, either within a county or defined radius. That way, we support local growers who transport their produce the shortest distance from plot to plate, and also help reduce the environmental damage potentially caused by shipping vegetables thousands of miles across the world.

A key advantage to seasonal eating is that you can enjoy vegetables when they are at their best and cheapest at the height of their natural harvest time. If there is a glut, it is worth buying them in quantity and freezing the excess to be enjoyed at other times of the year.

Another advantage is that vegetables eaten in season are a real culinary treat as opposed to a slightly monotonous year-round feature on the menu. The first asparagus, early new potatoes, young broad beans and peas are something to be eagerly relished after the relative bleakness of early spring. Tomatoes, courgettes and peppers are at their best in late summer, winter squash and pumpkins are a colourful reminder that autumn is on its way, while parsnips and Brussels sprouts come into their own after the first frosts.

Eating seasonally helps put us in touch with natural rhythms of the culinary calendar. And by limiting your choice to what is in season, you are also more likely to experiment with unfamiliar varieties that you might otherwise not add to the menu.

What's in season

The following lists are an approximate guide to availability since weather conditions vary according to region. With the exception of cultivated mushrooms, the lists refer to outdoor crops rather than those grown in polytunnels or under glass.

Spring

asparagus *(late spring)*

cabbage (red, white, spring, other green varieties)

carrots

cauliflower

celeriac

chard

garlic (fresh, wild) *(late spring)*

leeks *(early spring)*

mushrooms (wild morels, cultivated)

onions (red, white, salad/spring)

parsnips

potatoes *(late spring)*

radishes *(late spring)*

rocket *(late spring)*

shallots *(early spring)*

spinach

spring greens

sprouting broccoli *(early spring)*

squash

swede

watercress

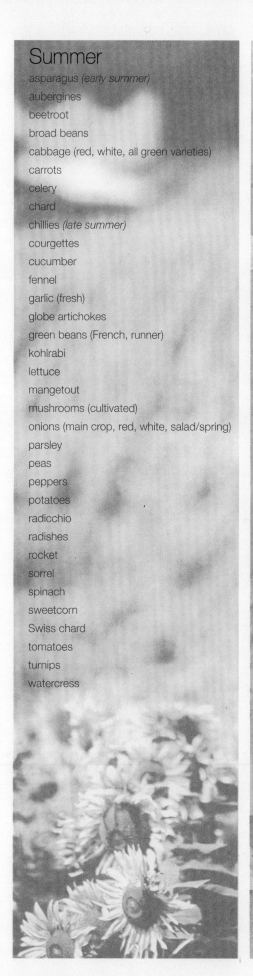

Summer

asparagus *(early summer)*
aubergines
beetroot
broad beans
cabbage (red, white, all green varieties)
carrots
celery
chard
chillies *(late summer)*
courgettes
cucumber
fennel
garlic (fresh)
globe artichokes
green beans (French, runner)
kohlrabi
lettuce
mangetout
mushrooms (cultivated)
onions (main crop, red, white, salad/spring)
parsley
peas
peppers
potatoes
radicchio
radishes
rocket
sorrel
spinach
sweetcorn
Swiss chard
tomatoes
turnips
watercress

Autumn

aubergines *(early autumn)*
beetroot
Brussels sprouts *(late autumn)*
borlotti beans (fresh)
broccoli
cabbage (red, white, Savoy, other green
   varieties)
carrots
cauliflower
celeriac
celery
chard
chicory
chillies *(early autumn)*
courgettes
cucumber
endive
globe artichokes
green beans (French, runner) *(early autumn)*
Jerusalem artichokes
kale
kohlrabi
leeks
lettuce
mushrooms (wild, cultivated)
onions (main crop, pickling, red, white,
   salad/spring)
oriental salad leaves
parsley
parsnips
peppers *(early autumn)*
potatoes
pumpkins
radicchio
radishes
rocket
shallots
sorrel
spinach
squash
swede
sweetcorn *(early autumn)*
sweet potatoes
Swiss chard
tomatoes
turnips
watercress
winter squash

Winter

Brussels sprouts
cabbage (red, white, Savoy, other green
   varieties)
carrots
cauliflower
celeriac
celery
chard
chicory
endive
Jerusalem artichokes
kale
leeks
mushrooms (cultivated)
onion (main crop, pickling, red, white)
parsnips
potatoes
radishes
radicchio
rocket
shallots
sprouting broccoli
swede
sweet potatoes
turnips
watercress

Storing Vegetables

From the moment of harvest, vegetables gradually start to deteriorate. Though they remain edible for a while, the flavour undergoes subtle changes, as does the texture, and they begin to lose valuable nutrients. Correct storage helps to slow down deterioration, so it is worth taking a few key principles on board.

Many vegetables benefit from the humidity of the refrigerator salad drawer, but others have different requirements. Tomatoes, for example, are best kept at room temperature since the chill of the refrigerator simply dulls the flavour. Similarly, the refrigerator is not a good place for onions, winter squash and starchy root vegetables. These are best kept in a dry, airy shed, a cool larder or a ventilated drawer.

Packaging is also important. It's a good idea to keep your vegetables in a brown paper bag, or a ventilated plastic bag when storing them in the refrigerator. This provides the slightly humid but well-ventilated atmosphere that many vegetables need. A sealed plastic bag is better for watercress and fragile leafy greens that need an enclosed moist environment.

Freezing

Freezing is an excellent way of preserving vegetables, especially a glut of home-grown ones. Most will keep for 9–12 months provided they are in peak condition.

Prior to freezing, vegetables should be blanched to destroy enzymes that would otherwise speed up deterioration. Once blanched, cool quickly under running water, then drain and dry well before packing. Some vegetables, such as celery and peppers, lose their crisp texture once thawed so are best used in stews and soups.

Vegetables that are worth freezing are indicated on this and the following pages, together with preparation tips and blanching times.

Vegetable fruits

Aubergines: Store in the refrigerator salad drawer for 3–4 days.

Avocados: Store hard fruits at room temperature; they will ripen in 2–7 days. Store ripe fruits in the refrigerator salad drawer for 2–3 days.

Chillies and peppers: Store in the refrigerator salad drawer for up to 1 week. For the best flavour, bring to room temperature before using. Once cut, wrap tightly in clingfilm and use within 24 hours.
To freeze: Halve lengthways and discard stalk and seeds. Grill halves for 5–8 minutes, or slice thickly and blanch for 3 minutes.

Courgettes: Store in the refrigerator salad drawer for 2–4 days.
To freeze: Trim and slice thickly. Blanch for 1 minute.

Cucumbers: Store in the refrigerator salad drawer for 3–4 days. Once cut, wrap tightly in clingfilm and use within 24 hours.

Pumpkins and winter squash: Store in a dry, airy shed for 2–6 months, or at room temperature for 2–3 weeks.
To freeze: Cut into wedges and discard skin and seeds. Roast until tender, or cut into chunks, blanch for 3 minutes, then purée.

Tomatoes: Store ripe fruit at room temperature for 1–2 days. If not quite ripe, leave to ripen, preferably on a sunny windowsill, for up to 1 week. Avoid storing in the refrigerator as the chill dulls the flavour.
To freeze: Chop and simmer in own juice for 5 minutes, then purée. Push through a sieve for a smoother purée.

Shoots

Asparagus: Trim the ends and place upright in a jug of water loosely covered with a plastic bag. Store in the refrigerator for 1–2 days.
To freeze: Divide into thick and thin stems. Trim woody ends. Blanch thick stems for 4 minutes, thin stems for 2 minutes.

Globe artichokes: Wrap tightly in clingfilm and store in the refrigerator salad drawer for 2–3 days.

Stems

Celery: Store in the plastic sleeve in the refrigerator salad drawer for up to 1 week. Once trimmed, wrap unused stems tightly in kitchen foil. Store for up to 3 days.

Fennel: Store in the refrigerator salad drawer for up to 4 days. Once cut, wrap tightly in clingfilm and use within 24 hours.

Roots

Beetroot: Remove leaves, leaving a small length of stem attached. Store in the refrigerator salad drawer for up to 1 week.

Carrots: Remove leaves, leaving a small length of stem attached. Store in the refrigerator salad drawer for up to 1 week. Store baby carrots for 1–2 days.
To freeze: Leave whole if small, slice thickly if large. Blanch for 3–5 minutes.

Celeriac: Store in a dry, airy shed for up to 2 weeks. Otherwise, wrap in clingfilm and store in the refrigerator salad drawer for up to 1 week.

Radishes: Remove leaves, leaving a short length of stem attached. Wrap in damp kitchen paper, unwashed. Store in a sealed plastic bag in the refrigerator salad drawer for up to 1 week.

Tubers

Jerusalem artichokes: Store away from light in a dry, airy shed for 3–4 weeks. Alternatively store in a cloth bag or paper sack in a well-ventilated drawer for up to 1 week.

Potatoes: Store away from light, in a dry, airy shed for 2–3 months. Alternatively, store in a cloth bag or paper sack in a well-ventilated drawer for up to 1 week.

Sweet potatoes: Store away from light in a dry, airy shed for 3–4 weeks. Alternatively, store in a cloth bag or paper sack in a well-ventilated drawer for up to 1 week.

Brassicas

Broccoli and cauliflower: Store in the refrigerator salad drawer for 2–3 days.
To freeze: Break into florets. Slice thick stems. Blanch for 3–5 minutes.

Brussels sprouts: Store in the refrigerator salad drawer for 1–2 days.
To freeze: Trim ends and make small cross cut in base. Blanch for 3–4 minutes.

Cabbage: Store uncut in the refrigerator salad drawer for up to 1 week. Once cut, wrap unused portion tightly in clingfilm and use within 1–2 days.

Chard: Wrap in damp kitchen paper, unwashed. Store in a sealed plastic bag in the refrigerator salad drawer for 1–2 days.

Kale: Trim tough stalks. Wrap in damp kitchen paper, unwashed. Store in a sealed plastic bag in the refrigerator salad drawer for 3–4 days.

Pak choi: Wrap in damp kitchen paper, unwashed. Store in a sealed plastic bag in the refrigerator salad drawer for 1–2 days.

Spinach: Wash and dry, then spread out on kitchen paper and roll up loosely. Store in a roomy sealed plastic bag in the refrigerator salad drawer for 1–2 days.
To freeze: Trim tough stalks. Blanch in small batches for 2 minutes. Squeeze out liquid before freezing.

Salad leaves

Chicory: Store in the refrigerator salad drawer for 2–3 days.

Lettuce, endive and radicchio: Store unwashed in the refrigerator salad drawer for 3–4 days. Alternatively, wash and dry, then spread out on kitchen paper and roll up loosely. Store in a roomy, sealed plastic bag in the refrigerator salad drawer for 1–2 days.

Rocket and miscellaneous small leaves: Wash and dry, then spread out on kitchen paper and roll up loosely. Store in a roomy, sealed plastic bag in the refrigerator salad drawer for 1–2 days.

Watercress: Wrap bunched watercress in damp kitchen paper. Store in a sealed plastic bag in the refrigerator salad drawer for 1–2 days.

Mushrooms

Cultivated and wild mushrooms: Store loosely wrapped in a brown paper bag in the refrigerator salad drawer for 1–2 days.

Onion family

Garlic: Store in a clay garlic pot or in a ventilated drawer or vegetable rack for 7–10 days.

Leeks: Store in the refrigerator salad drawer for up to 1 week.

Onions and shallots: Store yellow onions and shallots in a cool, airy shed for several weeks. Alternatively, store in a ventilated drawer or vegetable rack for up to 10 days. Store white, red and Spanish onions for no more than 5–7 days as they rot more quickly.

Spring onions: Store in the refrigerator salad drawer for up to 1 week.

Pods and seeds

Beansprouts: Store in a sealed plastic bag in the refrigerator salad drawer for 1–2 days.

Broad beans: Store unshelled in the refrigerator salad drawer for 2–3 days.
To freeze: Select small- to medium-sized beans. Shell and blanch for 3 minutes.

Green beans: Store in the refrigerator salad drawer for 3–4 days.
To freeze: Trim, remove strings if necessary. Cut French beans into lengths or leave whole. Slice runner beans. Blanch for 2–3 minutes.

Peas: Store unshelled in the refrigerator salad drawer, unpadded, for 1–2 days.
To freeze: Select young tender peas. Shell and blanch for 1–2 minutes.

Sweetcorn: Keep husks intact, and wrap in damp kitchen paper. Store in a sealed plastic bag in the refrigerator salad drawer for up to 24 hours.

Preparing Vegetables

Although many supermarkets now sell ready-prepared vegetables, it is far better to buy vegetables fresh and loose and to prepare them just before you need them. Wash or scrub everything, but do not leave vegetables soaking in water or their soluble nutrients will leach out. Similarly, do not cut or prepare vegetables too far in advance, as some vitamins, such as vitamin C, diminish once the cut surface is exposed to the air.

How to prepare peppers

1. Wash the peppers, then cut lengthways in half.
2. Remove and discard the green stalk.
3. Cut out the white membranes and any remaining seeds, then slice or chop as required.

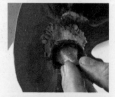

How to peel and deseed tomatoes

1. Cut the stalk end out of each tomato using a sharp knife. Cut a cross in the skin of each tomato. Bring a large pan of water to the boil, then add the tomatoes. Leave to stand for 5–10 seconds, or until the tomato skins begin to loose, then remove with a slotted spoon.
2. Place the tomatoes in a bowl of iced water to stop the cooking.
3. Drain the tomatoes and carefully remove the skins.
4. Cut the tomatoes into quarters, then remove and discard the seeds. Dice the flesh or cut into strips, as required.

How to chop onions

1. Peel the onion and cut in half lengthways.
2. Place the onion halves cut-side down on a chopping board. Cut the onion halves lengthways, taking care not to cut through the root.
3. Turn the blade of the knife so it is parallel with the board and slice the onion, again leaving the root end intact.
4. Grip the onion firmly, then turn the knife again and cut crossways across the original slices until you reach the root end.

How to prepare leeks

1. Remove and discard the root end from the leeks.
2. Trim the opposite end of the leeks, discarding the dark green leaves.
3. Peel off the outer layer of the leeks.
4. Wash the leeks under cold running water to remove any dirt, then slice or chop as required.

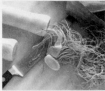

How to prepare a pumpkin or squash

1. Cut the pumpkin or squash crossways in half, then spoon the seeds into a bowl and set aside.
2. Cut the flesh into wedges and peel off the skin.
3. Remove and discard the stringy insides using a sharp knife.
4. Cut the pumpkin or squash wedges into 1-cm/½-inch chunks.
5. If wished, the seeds can be roasted at 160°C/325°F/Gas Mark 3 for 30 minutes. Sprinkle with salt before serving.

How to prepare celery

1. Remove and discard the root end of the celery and trim the leaf end.
2. Wash the celery sticks well under cold running water.
3. Remove the strings using a sharp knife or vegetable peeler, then slice or chop the celery as required.

How to prepare fennel

1. Remove and discard the root end of the fennel.
2. Peel off the outer layers.
3. Trim off the stalks and leaves. The leaves can be used as a garnish and the stalks may be used in sauces and stocks.
4. Slice the bulb in half through the root, then slice or chop the fennel as required.

How to prepare mushrooms

1. Trim the mushroom stalks, removing any dirt.
2. Wipe the mushrooms with a sheet of damp kitchen paper, then slice or chop as required.

How to prepare spinach

1. Wash the spinach under cold running water. Remove and discard any yellow leaves.
2. Remove and discard the stems.

Essential Cooking Techniques

While most vegetables can be eaten raw, there are numerous cooking techniques that will add interest and variety to your meals. You can maximize the flavour, colour and texture of the vegetables, while preserving as much of the essential vitamins and nutrients as possible.

Boiling

The traditional method of cooking vegetables is to use plenty of salted water and a large uncovered saucepan. This method is most suitable for sweetcorn, potatoes and other root vegetables. Although steaming is preferable when cooking green vegetables because they retain more nutrients, if you choose to boil them leave them uncovered; put the lid on and they lose their attractive bright green colour. Choose an appropriate size of saucepan for the quantity of vegetables so that the water can circulate, but use the minimum amount of water, cook for the briefest period and drain the vegetables immediately because boiling destroys water-soluble vitamins, such as B and C. Other soluble nutrients leach into the cooking water, so get into the habit of keeping the cooking water and using it as a base for soup or sauces.

Poaching

A less vigorous way to cook more delicate vegetables is to put them in boiling liquid (water, stock, wine or milk), then to simmer them gently over a low heat to retain their flavour, texture and shape.

Frying

Deep-frying is less popular these days, with concerns over the amount of fat in our diet. In fact, if the cooking temperature is correct, deep-fried foods are quickly sealed and absorb less oil than when they are shallow-fried. Coating vegetables in batter or in egg and breadcrumbs forms a crispy seal, which also reduces oil absorption. Deep-frying is a long-established cooking method for potatoes (chips) and also works well for aubergines and courgettes. Dry-frying in a frying pan or griddle pan or on a flat griddle plate is a healthier option that can be used for some vegetables.

Steaming

Less water comes into contact with vegetables when they are steamed rather than boiled, so they are crispy and retain more essential nutrients. Also, some vegetables – mangetout, leeks and courgettes – become limp and unappetizing if boiled. Steamed new potatoes are particularly delicious; try putting some fresh mint leaves under the potatoes to flavour them while they are steaming.

Braising

This cooking method requires only a very little water, and the saucepan is covered. The heat is much reduced and the cooking time greatly increased. You can start by browning the ingredients in a little oil or butter, then add water or other liquid before covering the saucepan. The small amount of liquid that remains at the end of the cooking will be sweet and flavoured – serve the vegetables with this juice and you gain all the nutrients. Onions, turnips, leeks, chicory, celery and fennel lend themselves to braising. Red cabbage is one of the brassicas that positively benefits from this long, slow method of cooking.

Stir-frying

This method of frying in a little oil over a very high heat has become widely popular. Stir-fried vegetables

retain far more of their nutritional value, flavour, texture and colour. They are thinly sliced and rapidly moved around in a hot wok to aid fast and even cooking. Most of us are familiar with stir-fried baby corn, mangetout, peppers, beansprouts and bamboo shoots, but the method is an equally good way to cook thinly sliced cauliflower, Brussels sprouts, cabbage and carrots.

Roasting

Traditionally, roasting vegetables meant cooking them in the fat dripping from a joint of meat. The far healthier option is to roast vegetables that have been lightly drizzled with olive oil in a roasting tin, to which you can add garlic and herbs for additional flavour. Squash, parsnips, potatoes, peppers, onions, tomatoes, asparagus and even beetroot are all delicious cooked in this way; their flavour is concentrated and the natural sweetness of the vegetables is accentuated.

Sautéeing and sweating

These methods use less oil than traditional shallow-frying and are longer, slower processes than stir-frying. Sautéeing is done in an uncovered frying pan; sweating in either a heavy-based lidded casserole or frying pan – water evaporating from the ingredients is trapped and falls back into the pan. Onions are often sweated to soften them without colouring.

Baking

Potatoes, onions and garlic can be baked 'dry' in their skins, while softer vegetables (such as peppers and tomatoes) can be stuffed with rice or other filling or wrapped in foil and baked.

Grilling and barbecuing

Grilling and barbecuing are both dry-heat cooking methods that are similar to each other, with the former cooking from the top and the latter from the bottom. The intense heat from a grill or barbecue is unsuitable for either delicate or dense vegetables, which become charred rather than cooked, but excellent for softer ones, such as onions, sweetcorn, peppers, aubergines and tomatoes. All vegetables need to be brushed with oil before being placed on the grill.

Cooking times

For maximum nutritional benefit, it makes sense to cook your vegetables for the least amount of time possible. Cut them the same size so that they look attractive and cook evenly. While potatoes have to be cooked right through, other root vegetables, such as carrots, are best served with a little 'bite' to them. Boil for less time or steam your vegetables and enjoy the extra crunch. Some vegetables – those with a high water content, such as spinach, celery or beansprouts – need only be blanched in boiling water for 30 seconds. For frying and stir-frying, ensure that the oil is properly hot before adding the vegetables. When time is short, try microwaving your vegetables. This method requires less liquid or fat, and results in shorter cooking times than conventional cooking.

Chapter 1
Vegetable Fruits

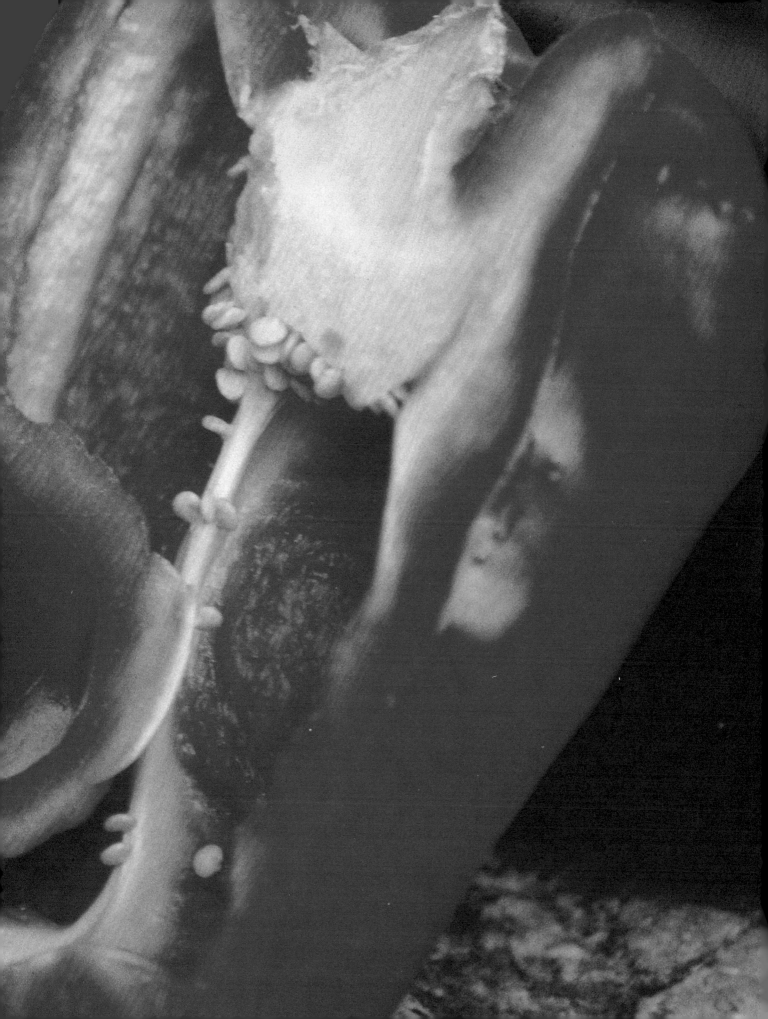

Directory of Vegetable Fruits

The vegetables in this group are technically fruits but are normally treated as vegetables. Vegetable fruits are incredibly versatile – they are suitable for the majority of cooking methods and some of them can also be eaten raw.

Aubergines

Known in the Middle East as 'poor man's caviar', aubergines give substance and flavour to spicy stews and tomato-based bakes. They can be roasted, grilled, or puréed into garlicky dips.

Avocados

With their rich, nutty flavour and buttery texture, avocados are ideal for eating raw. They are eaten straight from the shell, added to salads, or puréed with zesty seasonings to make guacamole or other dips. Avocados can also be baked, or used in a rich creamy soup.

Chillies

Chillies have a crucial role in many cuisines, particularly Mexican, Indian and Thai. There are hundreds of different types, ranging in potency from mildly piquant to blisteringly hot. Chillies can be fried, roasted or grilled, added to soups and stews, or used to perk up starchy vegetables, pulses and grain dishes.

Cucumbers

The cooling nature of cucumbers comes into its own in Indian and Middle Eastern cuisines. Here they are traditionally combined with yogurt and mint to make soothing sauces and dips to offset the heat of spicy dishes. Smooth-skinned types have tender skin and do not need peeling. Spiny ridge cucumbers have tough bitter skin that must be removed. Cucumbers are best eaten raw. They add colour and texture to salads and they also make excellent pickles.

Peppers

Peppers come in a spectrum of colours, starting off grassy green, then maturing to yellow, orange and vibrant red. Some varieties are rich purple or even chocolate brown. They all add substance and colour to many kinds of soups, salads, stews and stir-fries. They can also be stuffed with meat or rice, grilled as an hors d'oeuvre, or puréed for dips and sauces.

Tomatoes

There are now so many varieties from which to choose, from the sweet bite-sized cherry to the large, beefy slicing tomato. With its thick juicy flesh, the egg-shaped plum tomato is perfect for rich sauces, while sun-dried tomatoes add intense flavour to dips, sauces, soups and stews.

Summer squash

Courgettes are one of the best-known summer squash. They are at their best when small and young; the flavour diminishes and the seeds toughen as they grow older and larger. Extremely versatile, courgettes can be steamed, stir-fried, puréed, griddled and roasted, as well as used in soups and casseroles. Their deep yellow flowers are perfect for stuffing. If left to mature, courgettes will become marrows, which tend to be fleshy and watery but are perfect for stuffing and chutneys. Other popular summer squashes include pattypan and spaghetti squash.

Winter squash and pumpkins

Butternut squash is one of the most readily available winter types. A large, distinctively pear-shaped vegetable with a golden skin and orange flesh, it is equally delicious mashed, baked or roasted, or used in soups and stews. Pumpkins can be used in much the same way, though the flesh tends to be more watery and disintegrates easily. Small pumpkins have a sweeter, less fibrous flesh than the large ones, which are probably best kept for making lanterns at Halloween!

Tomato Bruschetta

Serves 4

ingredients
- 8 slices of rustic bread
- 4 garlic cloves, halved
- 8 plum tomatoes, peeled and diced
- extra virgin olive oil, for drizzling
- salt and pepper
- fresh basil leaves, to garnish

1 Preheat the grill. Lightly toast the bread on both sides. Rub each piece of toast with half a garlic clove and then return to the grill for a few seconds.

2 Divide the diced tomatoes among the toasts. Season to taste with salt and pepper and drizzle with oil. Serve immediately, garnished with basil leaves.

Polenta with Tomatoes & Garlic Sauce

Serves 4

ingredients

- 700 ml/1¼ pints vegetable stock or water
- 175 g/6 oz quick-cook polenta
- 25 g/1 oz butter
- 3 tbsp snipped fresh chives
- 2 tbsp chopped fresh flat-leaf parsley
- olive oil, for brushing
- 4 plum tomatoes, sliced
- salt and pepper

garlic sauce

- 2 thick slices of French bread, crusts removed
- 3 garlic cloves, chopped
- ½ tsp salt
- 115 g/4 oz walnut pieces
- 3 tbsp lemon juice
- 7 tbsp olive oil

1 Bring the stock to the boil in a large saucepan. Add the polenta and cook over a medium heat, stirring constantly, for 5 minutes, until it starts to come away from the sides of the pan.

2 Remove the pan from the heat and beat in the butter, chives and parsley and season to taste with pepper. Pour the polenta into an oiled dish and spread out evenly. Leave to cool and set.

3 To make the garlic sauce, tear the bread into pieces and place in a bowl. Cover with cold water and leave to soak for 10 minutes. Pound the garlic cloves with the salt to make a paste. Work in the walnuts. Squeeze out the bread, work it into the paste, then add the lemon juice. Stir in the oil until the sauce is thick and creamy. Transfer to a bowl, cover with clingfilm and set aside.

4 Brush a ridged griddle with oil and preheat. Cut the set polenta into wedges or rounds. Season the tomatoes with salt and pepper. When the griddle is hot, add the polenta and tomatoes, and cook for 4–5 minutes.

5 Divide the polenta and tomatoes among warmed plates and spoon over the garlic sauce. Serve immediately.

Avocado &
Almond Soup

Serves 4

ingredients
- 600 ml/1 pint water
- 1 onion, finely chopped
- 1 celery stick, finely chopped
- 1 carrot, grated
- 4 garlic cloves, chopped or crushed
- 1 bay leaf
- ½ tsp salt, or to taste
- 100 g/3½ oz ground almonds
- 2 ripe avocados (about 450 g/1 lb total weight)
- 3–4 tbsp lemon juice
- extra virgin olive oil, for drizzling
- snipped fresh chives, to garnish

1 Combine the water, onion, celery, carrot, garlic, bay leaf and salt in a pan. Bring to the boil, reduce the heat, cover and simmer for about 30 minutes, or until the vegetables are very tender.

2 Strain the mixture, reserving the liquid and the vegetables separately. Remove and discard the bay leaf.

3 Put the vegetables into a blender or food processor. Add the almonds and a small amount of the liquid and process to a very smooth purée, scraping down the sides as necessary. Add as much of the remaining liquid as the capacity of the blender or processor permits and process to combine. Scrape into a bowl, stir in any remaining liquid, cover and chill in the refrigerator until cold.

4 Cut the avocados in half, discard the stones and scoop the flesh into the blender or food processor. Add the cold soup base and process to a smooth purée, scraping down the sides as necessary. For a thinner consistency, add a few spoonfuls of cold water.

5 Add the lemon juice and season to taste with salt. Ladle into chilled bowls and drizzle with extra virgin olive oil. Serve immediately, garnished with chives.

Pasta Salad with
Chargrilled Peppers

Serves 4

ingredients
- 1 red pepper
- 1 orange pepper
- 280 g/10 oz dried conchiglie
- 5 tbsp extra virgin olive oil
- 2 tbsp lemon juice
- 2 tbsp pesto
- 1 garlic clove, finely chopped
- 3 tbsp shredded fresh basil leaves
- salt and pepper

1 Preheat the grill. Put the whole peppers on a baking tray and place under the hot grill, turning frequently, for 15 minutes, or until charred all over. Remove with tongs and place in a bowl. Cover with crumpled kitchen paper and reserve.

2 Meanwhile, bring a large saucepan of lightly salted water to the boil. Add the pasta, return to the boil and cook for 8–10 minutes, or until the pasta is tender but still firm to the bite.

3 Combine the oil, lemon juice, pesto and garlic in a large bowl, whisking well to mix. Drain the pasta, add it to the oil mixture while still hot and toss well. Reserve until required.

4 When the peppers are cool enough to handle, peel off the skins, then cut open and remove the seeds. Chop the flesh roughly and add to the pasta with the basil. Season to taste with salt and pepper and toss well. Serve.

Summer Vegetable &
Herb Tart

Serves 4–6

ingredients
- 2 red peppers
- 4 tbsp olive oil
- 350 g/12 oz ready-made puff pastry, thawed if frozen
- plain flour, for dusting
- 2 ripe but firm tomatoes, thinly sliced
- 250 g/9 oz ricotta cheese
- 100 g/3½ oz Parmesan cheese, grated
- 1 tsp fresh thyme leaves
- 1 tbsp snipped fresh chives
- salt and pepper

1 Preheat the oven to 200°C/400°F/ Gas Mark 6.

2 Remove the stalks and seeds from the red peppers and cut the flesh into thin strips. Transfer to a baking tray and drizzle with half the oil. Season to taste with salt and pepper and roast in the preheated oven for 20 minutes, or until soft. Remove from the oven and leave to cool while you prepare the tart case.

3 Roll the pastry out on a floured work surface and use to line a 23-cm/9-inch tart tin. Prick the base with a fork to prevent the pastry from puffing up.

4 Scatter the roasted peppers evenly over the base of the tart case, then arrange the tomato slices on top and season to taste with salt and pepper.

5 Beat the ricotta cheese in a bowl until smooth, then spoon over the vegetables. Sprinkle over the Parmesan cheese, thyme and chives, then drizzle over the remaining oil. Bake in the preheated oven for 20 minutes, or until the pastry and cheese topping are golden. Serve immediately, or leave to cool.

Ratatouille

Serves 4

ingredients
- 2 aubergines
- 4 courgettes
- 2 yellow peppers
- 2 red peppers
- 2 onions
- 2 garlic cloves
- 150 ml/5 fl oz olive oil
- 1 bouquet garni
- 3 large tomatoes, peeled,
  deseeded and roughly chopped
- salt and pepper

1 Roughly chop the aubergines and courgettes, and deseed and chop the peppers. Slice the onions and finely chop the garlic.

2 Heat the oil in a large saucepan. Add the onions and cook over a low heat, stirring occasionally, for 5 minutes, or until softened. Add the garlic and cook, stirring frequently for a further 2 minutes.

3 Add the aubergines, courgettes and peppers. Increase the heat to medium and cook, stirring occasionally, until the peppers begin to colour. Add the bouquet garni, reduce the heat, cover and simmer gently for 40 minutes.

4 Stir in the tomatoes and season to taste with salt and pepper. Re-cover the saucepan and simmer gently for a further 10 minutes. Remove and discard the bouquet garni. Serve warm or cold.

Chilli Tofu Tortillas

Serves 4

ingredients
- ½ tsp chilli powder
- 1 tsp paprika
- 2 tbsp plain flour
- 225 g/8 oz firm tofu, cut into 1-cm/½-inch pieces
- 2 tbsp vegetable oil
- 1 onion, finely chopped
- 1 garlic clove, crushed
- 1 large red pepper, deseeded and finely chopped
- 1 large ripe avocado
- 1 tbsp lime juice
- 4 tomatoes, peeled, deseeded and chopped
- 125 g/4½ oz Cheddar cheese, grated
- 8 soft flour tortillas
- 150 ml/5 fl oz soured cream
- salt and pepper
- pickled green jalapeño chillies, to serve

sauce
- 850 ml/1½ pints sugocasa (see page 52)
- 3 tbsp chopped fresh parsley
- 3 tbsp chopped fresh coriander

1 Preheat the oven to 190°C/375°F/Gas Mark 5. Mix the chilli powder, paprika, flour and salt and pepper to taste on a plate and use to coat the tofu pieces.

2 Heat the oil in a frying pan and gently fry the tofu for 3–4 minutes, until golden. Remove with a slotted spoon, drain on kitchen paper and set aside.

3 Add the onion, garlic and red pepper to the oil and fry for 2–3 minutes, until just soft. Drain and set aside.

4 Halve the avocado, peel and remove the stone. Slice lengthways, put in a bowl with the lime juice and toss to coat.

5 Add the tofu and the onion mixture and gently stir in the tomatoes and half the cheese. Spoon a little of the filling down the centre of each tortilla, top with a little soured cream and roll up.

6 Arrange the tortillas in a shallow ovenproof dish in a single layer.

7 To make the sauce, mix all the ingredients together. Spoon the sauce over the tortillas, sprinkle with the remaining cheese and bake in the preheated oven for 25 minutes, until the cheese is golden brown and bubbling.

8 Serve the tortillas immediately with the pickled jalapeño chillies.

Pasta all'Arrabbiata

Serves 4

ingredients
- 150 ml/5 fl oz dry white wine
- 1 tbsp sun-dried tomato purée
- 2 fresh red chillies
- 2 garlic cloves, finely chopped
- 350 g/12 oz dried tortiglioni
- 4 tbsp chopped fresh
  flat-leaf parsley
- salt and pepper
- pecorino cheese shavings,
  to garnish

sugocasa
- 5 tbsp extra virgin olive oil
- 450 g/1 lb plum tomatoes,
  chopped
- salt and pepper

1 For the sugocasa, heat the oil in a frying pan over a high heat until almost smoking. Add the tomatoes and cook, stirring frequently, for 2–3 minutes. Reduce the heat to low and cook gently for 20 minutes, or until very soft. Season to taste with salt and pepper. Using a wooden spoon, press through a non-metallic sieve into a saucepan.

2 Add the wine, sun-dried tomato purée, whole chillies and garlic to the sugocasa and bring to the boil. Reduce the heat and simmer gently.

3 Meanwhile, bring a large saucepan of lightly salted water to the boil. Add the pasta, return to the boil and cook for 8–10 minutes, until the pasta is tender but still firm to the bite.

4 Remove the chillies and taste the sauce. If you prefer a hotter flavour, chop some or all of the chillies and return to the saucepan. Check and adjust the seasoning, adding salt and pepper if needed, then stir in half the parsley.

5 Drain the pasta and transfer to a warmed serving bowl. Add the sauce and toss to coat. Sprinkle with the remaining parsley, garnish with the pecorino cheese shavings and serve immediately.

Stuffed Aubergines

Serves 4

ingredients
- 225 g/8 oz dried penne or other short pasta shapes
- 4 tbsp olive oil, plus extra for brushing
- 2 aubergines
- 1 large onion, chopped
- 2 garlic cloves, crushed
- 400 g/14 oz canned chopped tomatoes
- 2 tsp dried oregano
- 55 g/2 oz mozzarella cheese, thinly sliced
- 25 g/1 oz Parmesan cheese, grated
- 5 tbsp dried breadcrumbs
- salt and pepper

1 Preheat the oven to 200°C/400°C/ Gas Mark 6. Bring a large saucepan of lightly salted water to the boil. Add the pasta and 1 tablespoon of the oil, return to the boil and cook for 8–10 minutes, or until the pasta is tender but still firm to the bite. Drain, return to the pan, cover and keep warm.

2 Cut the aubergines in half lengthways and score around the inside with a sharp knife, being careful not to pierce the skins. Scoop out the flesh with a spoon. Brush the insides with oil. Chop the flesh and set aside.

3 Heat the remaining oil in a frying pan. Fry the onion over a low heat for 5 minutes, until soft. Add the garlic and fry for 1 minute. Add the chopped aubergine and fry, stirring frequently, for 5 minutes. Add the tomatoes and oregano and season to taste with salt and pepper. Bring to the boil and simmer for 10 minutes, until thickened. Remove the pan from the heat and stir in the pasta.

4 Brush a baking tray with oil and arrange the aubergine shells in a single layer. Divide half of the tomato and pasta mixture among them. Scatter over the mozzarella cheese, then pile the remaining tomato and pasta mixture on top. Mix the Parmesan cheese and breadcrumbs and sprinkle over the top, patting lightly into the mixture.

5 Bake in the preheated oven for about 25 minutes, or until the topping is golden brown. Serve immediately.

Aubergine Curry

Serves 2

ingredients

- 2 aubergines, cut into 2-cm/¾-inch cubes
- 2 tbsp groundnut or vegetable oil, plus extra for deep-frying
- 1 bunch of spring onions, roughly chopped
- 2 garlic cloves, chopped
- 2 red peppers, deseeded and cut into 2-cm/¾-inch squares
- 3 courgettes, thickly sliced
- 400 ml/14 fl oz canned coconut milk
- 2 tbsp Thai red curry paste
- large handful of fresh coriander, chopped, plus extra sprigs to garnish
- cooked rice, to serve

1 Heat enough oil for deep-frying in a wok or a deep saucepan to 180–190°C/350–375°F, or until a cube of bread browns in 30 seconds. Add the aubergine cubes, in batches, and cook for 45 seconds–1 minute, until crisp and brown all over. Remove with a slotted spoon and drain on kitchen paper.

2 Heat the 2 tablespoons of oil in a separate wok or large frying pan, add the spring onions and garlic and stir-fry over a medium–high heat for 1 minute. Add the peppers and courgettes and stir-fry for 2–3 minutes.

3 Add the coconut milk and curry paste and bring gently to the boil, stirring occasionally. Add the aubergines and chopped coriander, reduce the heat and simmer for 2–3 minutes.

4 Serve immediately with rice, garnished with coriander sprigs.

Curried Courgette Soup

Serves 4

ingredients
- 10 g/¼ oz butter
- 1 large onion, finely chopped
- 900 g/2 lb courgettes, sliced
- 450 ml/16 fl oz vegetable stock
- 1 tsp curry powder
- 125 ml/4 fl oz soured cream, plus extra to serve
- salt and pepper

1 Melt the butter in a large saucepan over a medium heat. Add the onion and cook for about 3 minutes, until it begins to soften.

2 Add the courgettes, stock and curry powder, and season to taste with salt. Bring the soup to the boil, reduce the heat, cover and cook gently for about 25 minutes, until the vegetables are tender.

3 Allow the soup to cool slightly, then transfer to a food processor or blender, working in batches if necessary. Process the soup until just smooth, but still with green flecks. (If using a food processor, strain off the cooking liquid and reserve. Process the soup solids with enough cooking liquid to moisten them, then combine with the remaining liquid.)

4 Return the soup to the rinsed-out saucepan and stir in the soured cream. Reheat gently over a low heat just until hot. (Do not boil.)

5 Taste and adjust the seasoning, adding salt and pepper if needed. Ladle into warmed bowls, top with a spoonful of soured cream and serve.

Courgette & Basil Risotto

Serves 4

ingredients

- 1.5 litres/2¾ pints vegetable stock
- 4 tbsp basil-flavoured extra virgin olive oil, plus extra for drizzling
- 4 courgettes, diced
- 1 yellow pepper, deseeded and diced
- 2 garlic cloves, finely chopped
- 1 large onion, finely chopped
- 400 g/14 oz risotto rice
- 4 tbsp dry white vermouth
- 2 tbsp unsalted butter
- large handful of fresh basil leaves, torn, plus extra to garnish
- 85 g/3 oz Parmesan cheese, grated
- salt and pepper

1 Bring the stock to the boil, then reduce the heat and keep simmering gently over a low heat while you are cooking the risotto.

2 Heat half the oil in a large frying pan over a high heat. When very hot, but not smoking, add the courgettes and yellow pepper and stir-fry for 3 minutes, until lightly golden. Stir in the garlic and cook for a further 30 seconds. Transfer to a plate and set aside.

3 Heat the remaining oil in a deep saucepan over a medium heat. Add the onion and cook, stirring occasionally, for about 2 minutes, until soft. Add the rice and cook, stirring frequently, for about 2 minutes, until the rice is translucent and well coated with the oil.

4 Pour in the vermouth; it will bubble and steam rapidly and evaporate almost immediately.

5 Gradually add the hot stock, a ladleful at a time, stirring constantly. Add more stock as the rice absorbs each addition. Increase the heat so the liquid bubbles. Cook for 20–25 minutes, or until all the liquid has been absorbed and the rice is creamy but still firm to the bite.

6 Stir in the courgette mixture with any juices, the butter, basil and Parmesan cheese. Season to taste with salt and pepper. Drizzle with a little oil and garnish with basil. Serve immediately.

Summer Courgette
Ribbon Salad

Serves 4–6

ingredients
- 2 green courgettes
- 2 yellow courgettes
- 1 large carrot
- 115 g/4 oz radishes, thinly sliced
- 4–6 spring onions, chopped
- 2–3 tbsp shredded fresh basil leaves

dressing
- 4 tbsp extra virgin olive oil
- 1 tbsp lemon juice (or white wine vinegar)
- ½-1 tsp Dijon mustard
- 1 small garlic clove, crushed (optional)
- salt and pepper

1 To make the dressing, place the oil, lemon juice, mustard, garlic, if using, and salt and pepper to taste in a small bowl and whisk together until thoroughly mixed. Set aside.

2 Using a vegetable peeler, cut the green and yellow courgettes into long, thin ribbons, avoiding the seeds in the centre (discard the seedy cores). Place in a salad bowl.

3 Repeat with the carrot to make long, thin ribbons, then add these to the bowl together with the radishes, spring onions and basil. Toss gently to mix.

4 Give the dressing a quick whisk, then drizzle over the salad and toss gently to coat. Serve immediately.

Roasted Butternut Squash

Serves 4

ingredients

- 1 butternut squash, about 450 g/1 lb
- 1 onion, chopped
- 2–3 garlic cloves, crushed
- 4 small tomatoes, chopped
- 85 g/3 oz chestnut mushrooms, chopped
- 85 g/3 oz canned butter beans, drained, rinsed and roughly chopped
- 1 courgette, about 115 g/4 oz, grated
- 1 tbsp chopped fresh oregano, plus extra to garnish
- 2 tbsp tomato purée
- 300 ml/10 fl oz water
- 4 spring onions, chopped
- 1 tsp hot pepper sauce
- pepper

1 Preheat the oven to 190°C/375°F/ Gas Mark 5. Prick the squash all over with a skewer, then roast in the preheated oven for 40 minutes, or until tender. Remove from the oven and leave until cool enough to handle.

2 Cut the squash in half lengthways and scoop out and discard the seeds, then scoop out some of the flesh, leaving a 1-cm/½-inch border all around. Chop the scooped-out flesh and put in a bowl. Place the squash halves side by side in a large roasting tin.

3 Add the onion, garlic, tomatoes and mushrooms to the squash flesh in the bowl. Add the butter beans, courgette, oregano and pepper to taste and mix well. Spoon the filling into the two squash halves, packing it down as firmly as possible.

4 Mix the tomato purée with the water, spring onions and hot pepper sauce in a small bowl and pour around the squash.

5 Cover loosely with a large sheet of foil and bake for 30 minutes, or until piping hot. Serve in warmed bowls, garnished with oregano.

Penne with Pumpkin Sauce

Serves 4

ingredients
- 55 g/2 oz unsalted butter
- 115 g/4 oz white onions or shallots, very finely chopped
- 800 g/1 lb 12 oz pumpkin
- freshly gratead nutmeg
- 350 g/12 oz dried penne
- 200 ml/7 fl oz single cream
- 4 tbsp grated Parmesan cheese
- 2 tbsp chopped fresh flat-leaf parsley
- salt and pepper

1 Melt the butter in a heavy-based saucepan over a low heat. Add the onions, sprinkle with a little salt, cover and cook, stirring frequently, for 25–30 minutes.

2 Scoop out and discard the pumpkin seeds. Peel and finely chop the flesh. Tip the pumpkin into the saucepan and season to taste with nutmeg. Cover and cook over a low heat, stirring occasionally, for 45 minutes.

3 Meanwhile, bring a large saucepan of lightly salted water to the boil. Add the pasta, return to the boil and cook for 8–10 minutes, or until the pasta is tender but still firm to the bite. Drain thoroughly, reserving about 150 ml/5 fl oz of the cooking liquid.

4 Stir the cream, cheese and parsley into the pumpkin sauce and season to taste with salt and pepper. If the mixture seems a little too thick, add some or all of the reserved cooking liquid and stir. Tip in the pasta and toss well. Serve immediately.

Pumpkin Chestnut Risotto

Serves 4

ingredients
- 1 litre/1¾ pints vegetable stock
- 1 tbsp olive oil
- 40 g/1½ oz butter
- 1 small onion, finely chopped
- 225 g/8 oz pumpkin, diced
- 225 g/8 oz chestnuts, cooked and shelled
- 280 g/10 oz risotto rice
- 150 ml/5 fl oz dry white wine
- 1 tsp crumbled saffron threads (optional)
- 85 g/3 oz Parmesan cheese, grated, plus extra to serve
- salt and pepper

1 Bring the stock to the boil, then reduce the heat and keep simmering gently over a low heat while you are cooking the risotto.

2 Heat the oil with 25 g/1 oz of the butter in a deep saucepan over a medium heat until the butter has melted. Stir in the onion and pumpkin and cook, stirring occasionally, for 5 minutes, or until the onion is soft and starting to turn golden and the pumpkin begins to colour. Roughly chop the chestnuts and add to the mixture. Stir thoroughly to coat.

3 Reduce the heat, add the rice and mix to coat in oil and butter. Cook, stirring constantly, for 2–3 minutes, or until the grains are translucent. Add the wine and cook, stirring constantly, for 1 minute until it has reduced. If using the saffron threads, dissolve them in 4 tablespoons of the hot stock and add the liquid to the rice after the wine has been absorbed. Cook, stirring constantly, until the liquid has been absorbed.

4 Gradually add the hot stock, a ladleful at a time, stirring constantly. Add more liquid as the rice absorbs each addition. Increase the heat to medium so that the liquid bubbles. Cook for 20 minutes, or until all the liquid has been absorbed and the rice is creamy but still firm to the bite.

5 Remove the risotto from the heat and add the remaining butter. Mix well, then stir in the Parmesan until it melts. Adjust the seasoning, adding salt and pepper if needed. Spoon the risotto onto warmed plates and serve immediately, sprinkled with Parmesan.

Chapter 2
Shoots, Stems, Roots & Tubers

Directory of Shoots, Stems, Roots & Tubers

The vegetables in this group grow either below the soil or on the surface above. Between them they form the base for all kinds of dishes from summery starters and salads to hearty soups and stews.

Asparagus

There are three main types of asparagus: white, purple and green. The fat, mildly flavoured, white variety is harvested as soon as the shoots start to poke through the soil. Purple and green asparagus are allowed to grow taller. The purple is tastier than the white, while the green type has the most pronounced flavour. Snap off the inedible woody end before briefly steaming, boiling, griddling or roasting.

Carrots and beetroot

When buying carrots and beetroot, remember that the smaller ones are sweeter. Raw carrots and beetroot can be grated into salads or used to make relishes. Roasting them intensifies their sweetness and both work well in soups.

Celeriac

Celeriac is a knobbly root with a flavour reminiscent of celery. Peel and grate raw into salads, steam, bake or combine with potatoes to make a delicious mash.

Celery

Celery lends a crunchy texture to salads and also makes a good base for soups and stews. Green celery is available all year round, and white is available in winter. Choose stems that are very firm and rigid, but don't forget the leaves, which have a tangy flavour and can be added to stocks. Celery hearts can also be braised.

Fennel

Fennel has a mild aniseed flavour, which is most potent when eaten raw – thinly sliced in a salad, for example. Roasting fennel (cut into wedges) tempers the flavour and adds a delicious sweetness. Fennel also goes well with many traditional Mediterranean flavours, such as tomatoes, olive oil, garlic and basil.

Globe artichokes

The distinguished globe artichoke has an exquisite flavour and is great fun to eat: simply boil the heads, remove the hairy choke, then detach each leaf and dip into garlic butter, mayonnaise or a vinaigrette dressing. The tastiest part is the fleshy base below the leaves. Cut it up and eat using a knife and fork.

Jerusalem artichokes

These small, knobbly tubers have a mild, nutty flavour and are delicious roasted, fried or transformed into soup. Scrub rather than peel before use.

Potatoes

There are hundreds of potato varieties with different textures, which lend themselves to particular cooking methods. Waxy potatoes, such as Charlotte, are very good for serving boiled or in salads, while floury varieties, such as Maris Piper, lend themselves to roasting, baking and mashing.

Radishes

Most well-known are the small red-skinned type, but there are other varieties including the large black-skinned radish and the more mildly flavoured white 'mooli' or daikon. With their crisp peppery flesh, radishes are delicious added to salads, or dipped in sea salt flakes and eaten on their own as a snack.

Sweet potatoes

These torpedo-shaped tubers have an orange or white flesh (the former is richer in beta carotene). When cooked, the white-fleshed variety has a drier texture, but both are good roasted, mashed or baked.

Asparagus with Lemon Butter Sauce

Serves 4

ingredients
- 800 g/1 lb 12 oz asparagus spears, trimmed
- 1 tbsp olive oil
- salt and pepper

sauce
- juice of ½ lemon
- 2 tbsp water
- 100 g/3½ oz butter, diced
- pepper

1 Preheat the oven to 200°C/400°F/ Gas Mark 6.

2 Lay the asparagus spears out in a single layer on a large baking tray. Drizzle over the oil, season to taste with salt and pepper and roast in the preheated oven for 10 minutes, or until just tender.

3 Meanwhile, make the sauce. Pour the lemon juice into a saucepan and add the water. Heat for a minute or so, then slowly add the butter, a little at a time, stirring constantly until it has all been incorporated. Season to taste with pepper and serve immediately with the asparagus.

Asparagus & Sun-dried
Tomato Risotto

Serves 4

ingredients
- 1 litre/1¾ pints vegetable stock
- 1 tbsp olive oil
- 40 g/1½ oz butter
- 1 small onion, finely chopped
- 6 sun-dried tomatoes, thinly sliced
- 280 g/10 oz risotto rice
- 150 ml/5 fl oz dry white wine
- 225 g/8 oz fresh asparagus spears, cooked
- 85 g/3 oz Parmesan cheese, grated, plus extra to garnish
- salt and pepper
- grated lemon rind, to garnish

1 Bring the stock to the boil in a saucepan, then reduce the heat and keep simmering gently over a low heat while you are cooking the risotto.

2 Heat the oil with 25 g/1 oz of the butter in a deep saucepan over a medium heat until the butter has melted.

3 Stir in the onion and sun-dried tomatoes and cook, stirring occasionally, for 5 minutes, until the onion is soft and starting to turn golden. Do not brown.

4 Reduce the heat, add the rice and mix to coat in oil and butter. Cook, stirring constantly, for 2–3 minutes, or until the grains are translucent. Add the wine and cook, stirring constantly, until it has reduced.

5 Gradually add the hot stock, a ladleful at a time. Stir constantly and add more liquid as the rice absorbs each addition. Increase the heat to medium so that the liquid bubbles. Cook for 20 minutes, or until all the liquid is absorbed and the rice is creamy but still firm to the bite.

6 While the risotto is cooking, cut most of the asparagus into pieces about 2.5 cm/1 inch long. Set aside several asparagus tips for garnishing the finished dish. Carefully fold the remaining asparagus into the risotto for the last 5 minutes of cooking time.

7 Remove the risotto from the heat and add the remaining butter. Mix well, then stir in the Parmesan until it melts. Season to taste with salt and pepper. Spoon the risotto into individual warmed serving dishes and garnish with reserved asparagus tips. Sprinkle some Parmesan and lemon rind on top and serve.

Baked Celery with Cream

Serves 4

ingredients
- 1 head of celery
- ½ tsp ground cumin
- ½ tsp ground coriander
- 1 garlic clove, crushed
- 1 red onion, thinly sliced
- 50 g/1¾ oz pecan nuts, halved
- 150 ml/5 fl oz vegetable stock
- 150 ml/5 fl oz single cream
- 50 g/1¾ oz fresh wholemeal breadcrumbs
- 25 g/1 oz Parmesan cheese, grated
- salt and pepper

1 Preheat the oven to 200°C/400°F/ Gas Mark 6. Trim the celery and cut into matchsticks. Place the celery in an ovenproof dish with the cumin, coriander, garlic, onion and pecan nuts.

2 Mix the stock and cream together in a jug and pour over the vegetables. Season to taste with salt and pepper. Mix the breadcrumbs and cheese together in a small bowl and sprinkle over the top to cover the vegetables.

3 Cook in the preheated oven for 40 minutes, or until the vegetables are tender and the top is crispy. Serve immediately.

Globe Artichokes with Chive Mayonnaise

Serves 4

ingredients
- 4 globe artichokes
- 1 lemon, halved
- 2 eggs
- 2 egg yolks
- ¼ tsp mustard powder
- 225 ml/8 fl oz sunflower oil
- 4 tbsp snipped fresh chives, plus a few longer pieces to garnish
- salt and pepper

1 Using a very sharp knife, slice the stalks and tips from the artichokes. Rub the cut surfaces with a lemon half to prevent blackening. Trim the tips of the remaining leaves with scissors and rub with the lemon half. Place the artichokes in a bowl of water to which you have added the juice of one of the lemon halves. Set aside the remaining lemon half.

2 Bring a saucepan of water to a boil. Add the artichokes, weighing them down with a heatproof plate to keep them submerged. Bring back to a boil, then boil for 30–40 minutes. Drain and place upside down on a plate to cool.

3 Meanwhile, put the whole eggs in a small saucepan and cover with cold water. Bring to a boil, and boil for 5 minutes. Drain and leave to cool. Peel the shells from the boiled eggs and slice in half lengthways. Separate the yolks from the whites and put them in a mixing bowl with the raw egg yolks.

4 Beat the yolks for 1 minute until smooth and sticky. Beat in the mustard powder, a pinch of salt and a teaspoon of juice from the reserved lemon half. Add the oil, drop by drop, beating with each addition. Once the mixture starts to thicken, add the oil in a continuous thin stream, beating constantly. Thin with a little more lemon juice when all the oil is used up. Stir in the snipped chives and season with salt and pepper. Add more lemon juice if necessary.

5 Using a pointed teaspoon, scoop out the hairy 'choke' from the middle of the artichokes. To serve, place the artichokes on individual plates with the sauce to one side. Garnish with 2–3 long pieces of chive.

Jerusalem Artichoke Soup

Serves 4–6

ingredients
- 55 g/2 oz butter
- 2 onions, chopped
- 675 g/1 lb 8 oz Jerusalem artichokes, peeled and sliced
- 850 ml/1½ pints vegetable stock
- 300 ml/10 fl oz milk
- salt and pepper

croûtons
- 2 slices of day-old white bread, crusts removed
- 4 tbsp vegetable oil

1 To make the croûtons, cut the bread into 1-cm/½-inch cubes. Heat the oil in a frying pan and fry the croûtons in a single layer, tossing occasionally, until they are golden brown and crisp. Remove the pan from the heat and spoon out the croûtons onto kitchen paper to drain.

2 Melt the butter in a large saucepan over a medium heat, add the onions and cook until soft.

3 Add the Jerusalem artichokes and mix well with the butter, cover the saucepan and cook slowly over a low heat for about 10 minutes. Pour in the stock, bring to the boil, then reduce the heat and simmer, covered, for 20 minutes.

4 Remove from the heat and liquidize the soup in the saucepan using a hand-held stick blender, if you have one. Alternatively, pour into a blender, in batches if necessary, process until smooth and return to the rinsed-out saucepan. Stir in the milk and season to taste with salt and pepper.

5 Heat the soup until hot, ladle into warmed bowls and serve with the crispy croûtons.

Fennel Fritters with Red Pepper Mayonnaise

Serves 6

ingredients
- 3 fennel bulbs, trimmed
- 100 g/3½ oz stale white breadcrumbs
- 100 g/3½ oz Parmesan cheese, finely grated
- 2 tsp fennel seeds (optional)
- 1 egg, beaten
- sunflower oil, for shallow-frying
- salt and pepper
- lemon wedges, to serve

red pepper mayonnaise
- 2 red peppers
- 1 egg
- 1 tsp Dijon mustard
- 2–3 tbsp white wine vinegar
- pinch of salt
- 300 ml/10 fl oz sunflower oil
- 2 fresh red chillies, deseeded and chopped
- pepper

1 First make the mayonnaise. Using tongs, carefully hold each red pepper in turn over a high gas flame, turning frequently, for 8–10 minutes, or until blackened all over. Alternatively, preheat the oven to 220°C/425°F/Gas Mark 7. Put the red peppers on a baking tray and cook in the preheated oven, turning frequently, for 10–15 minutes, or until blackened all over.

2 Put the peppers in a polythene bag, seal and leave to cool. Peel off the charred skins and remove the seeds.

3 Put the egg, mustard, vinegar and salt in a blender and process to combine. With the motor running, slowly trickle in about one third of the oil. Once the mixture starts to thicken, add the remaining oil more quickly. When all the oil is incorporated, add the chillies and roasted peppers and process until smooth. Season to taste with pepper, then cover and chill in the refrigerator until required.

4 Cook the fennel bulbs in a large saucepan of salted boiling water for 15 minutes, or until almost tender – the exact cooking time will depend on their size. Drain and leave to cool, then carefully slice.

5 Mix the breadcrumbs and Parmesan cheese together, stir in the fennel seeds, if using, and season to taste with salt and pepper. Transfer the breadcrumb mixture to a large plate. Put the egg in a shallow dish. Coat the fennel slices in the egg and press the breadcrumb mixture firmly onto both sides.

6 Cover the base of a large frying pan with oil to a depth of about 1 cm/½ inch. Heat over a medium heat, add the fennel slices and cook, turning once, until golden brown. Remove and drain on kitchen paper. Serve immediately with the red pepper mayonnaise and lemon wedges to squeeze over.

Potato & Fennel Bake

Serves 6

ingredients
- 1 kg/2 lb 4 oz potatoes
- 2–3 fennel bulbs
- 4 tbsp olive oil
- 1 onion, finely chopped
- 2 garlic cloves, crushed
- 4 fresh sage leaves
- 150 ml/5 fl oz dry white wine
- salt and pepper

1 Preheat the oven to 200°C/400°F/ Gas Mark 6. Peel and finely slice the potatoes. Trim and finely slice the fennel.

2 Brush a large gratin dish with half the oil. Layer half the potato slices in the base of the prepared dish and season well with salt and pepper. Scatter over half the onion and garlic and cover with the fennel. Scatter over the remaining onion and garlic and season to taste again with salt and pepper. Tuck the sage leaves into the vegetables. Finish with a neat layer of the potato slices and season to taste again with salt and pepper.

3 Pour over the wine and drizzle over the remaining oil. Cover the dish with foil and bake in the preheated oven for 30 minutes.

4 Remove the foil and bake for a further 20–30 minutes, until the potatoes are brown and crisp.

Beetroot Salad

Serves 4–6

ingredients
- 900 g/2 lb raw beetroots
- 4 tbsp extra virgin olive oil
- 1½ tbsp red wine vinegar
- 2 garlic cloves, finely chopped
- 2 spring onions, very finely chopped
- salt

1 Carefully remove the roots from the beetroots without cutting into the skin, then cut off all but 2.5 cm/1 inch of the stalks. Gently rub the beetroots under cold running water, without splitting the skins, to remove any dirt.

2 Put the beetroots in a saucepan with water to cover and bring to the boil. Cover, reduce the heat slightly and cook for 25–40 minutes, depending on the size, until the largest beetroot is tender when pierced with a skewer or knife.

3 Meanwhile, put the oil, vinegar, garlic, spring onions and salt to taste in a jar with a screw-top lid and shake until emulsified, then set aside.

4 Drain the beetroots and rinse under cold running water until cool enough to handle, then peel away the skins. Thickly chop or slice the beetroots, then put in a bowl and pour over the dressing. Cover and chill in the refrigerator for at least 1 hour.

5 To serve, gently toss the salad and transfer to a serving bowl.

Bortsch

Serves 6

ingredients
- 1 onion
- 55 g/2 oz butter
- 350 g/12 oz raw beetroots, cut into thin batons, and 1 raw beetroot, grated
- 1 carrot, cut into thin batons
- 3 celery sticks, thinly sliced
- 2 tomatoes, peeled, deseeded and chopped
- 1.4 litres/2½ pints vegetable stock
- 1 tbsp white wine vinegar
- 1 tbsp sugar
- 2 tbsp snipped fresh dill
- 115 g/4 oz white cabbage, shredded
- 150 ml/5 fl oz soured cream
- salt and pepper
- crusty bread, to serve

1 Slice the onion into rings. Melt the butter in a large heavy-based saucepan. Add the onion and cook over a low heat, stirring occasionally, for 3–5 minutes, or until softened. Add the beetroot batons, carrot, celery and tomatoes and cook, stirring frequently, for 4–5 minutes.

2 Add the stock, vinegar, sugar and 1 tablespoon of the dill into the saucepan. Season to taste with salt and pepper. Bring to the boil, reduce the heat and simmer for 35–40 minutes, or until the vegetables are tender.

3 Stir in the cabbage, cover and simmer for 10 minutes. Stir in the grated beetroot, with any juices, and cook for a further 10 minutes. Ladle into warmed bowls. Top with the soured cream, sprinkle with the remaining dill and serve with crusty bread.

Sweet Potato Ravioli with Sage Butter

Serves 4

ingredients
- 400 g/14 oz type 00 pasta flour
- 4 eggs, beaten
- semolina, for dusting
- salt

filling
- 500 g/1 lb 2 oz sweet potatoes
- 3 tbsp olive oil
- 1 large onion, finely chopped
- 1 garlic clove, crushed
- 1 tsp chopped fresh thyme
- 2 tbsp runny honey
- salt and pepper

sage butter
- 50 g/1¾ oz butter
- 1 bunch of fresh sage leaves, finely chopped, plus extra leaves to garnish

1 To make the pasta dough, sift the flour into a large bowl or food processor. Add the eggs and bring the mixture together or process to make a soft but not sticky dough. Turn out onto a work surface lightly dusted with semolina and knead for 4–5 minutes, until smooth. Cover with clingfilm and chill in the refrigerator for at least 30 minutes.

2 For the filling, peel the sweet potatoes and cut into chunks. Cook in a saucepan of boiling water for 20 minutes, or until tender. Drain and mash.

3 Heat the oil in a frying pan over a medium heat, add the onion and cook, stirring frequently, for 4–5 minutes, until softened but not coloured. Stir the onion into the mashed potatoes and add the garlic and thyme. Drizzle with the honey and season to taste with salt and pepper. Set aside.

4 Using a pasta machine, roll the pasta out to a thickness of about 1 mm/ 1/32 inch (or use a rolling pin on a work surface lightly dusted with semolina).

5 Cut the pasta in half. Place teaspoonfuls of the filling at evenly spaced intervals across half of the pasta. Brush around the filling with a small amount of water and cover with the second half of the pasta. Press lightly around the filling to seal and cut into squares with a sharp knife or pastry wheel. Lay the ravioli out on a sheet of greaseproof paper that has been lightly dusted with semolina.

6 Bring a large saucepan of salted water to the boil and drop in the ravioli. Cook for 2–3 minutes, until the pasta rises to the surface and is tender but still firm to the bite.

7 Meanwhile, for the sage butter, melt the butter with the chopped sage in a small saucepan over a low heat.

8 Drain the ravioli and immediately toss with the sage butter. Serve immediately, garnished with sage leaves.

Roasted Potato Wedges
with Shallots & Rosemary

Serves 4

ingredients
- 1 kg/2 lb 4 oz small potatoes
- 6 tbsp olive oil
- 2 fresh rosemary sprigs
- 150 g/5½ oz baby shallots
- 2 garlic cloves, sliced
- salt and pepper

1 Preheat the oven to 200°C/400°F/ Gas Mark 6. Peel and cut each potato into 8 thick wedges. Put the potatoes in a large saucepan of lightly salted water and bring to the boil. Reduce the heat and simmer for 5 minutes.

2 Heat the oil in a large roasting tin on the hob. Drain the potatoes well and add to the roasting tin. Strip the leaves from the rosemary sprigs, chop finely and sprinkle over the potatoes.

3 Roast the potatoes in the preheated oven for 35 minutes, turning twice during cooking. Add the shallots and garlic and roast for a further 15 minutes, until golden brown. Season to taste with salt and pepper.

4 Transfer to a warmed serving dish and serve immediately.

Colcannon

Serves 3–4

ingredients
- 225 g/8 oz green or white cabbage
- 6 spring onions, cut into 5-mm/¼-inch slices
- salt and pepper

mashed potatoes
- 450 g/1 lb floury potatoes, cut into chunks
- 55 g/2 oz butter
- 150 ml/5 fl oz single cream
- salt and pepper

1 To make the mashed potatoes, cook the potatoes in a large saucepan of boiling salted water for 15–20 minutes. Drain well and mash with a potato masher until smooth. Season to taste with salt and pepper, add the butter and cream and stir well. The potato should be very soft.

2 Meanwhile, cut the cabbage into quarters, remove and discard the centre stalk and shred the leaves finely.

3 Cook the cabbage in a large saucepan of boiling salted water for just 1–2 minutes, until it is soft. Drain thoroughly.

4 Mix the potato and cabbage together and stir in the spring onions. Season well with salt and pepper. Serve immediately.

Potato Fritters with Onion & Tomato Relish

Serves 8

ingredients

- 55 g/2 oz wholemeal flour
- ½ tsp ground coriander
- ½ tsp cumin seeds
- ¼ tsp chilli powder
- ½ tsp turmeric
- ¼ tsp salt
- 1 egg
- 3 tbsp milk
- 350 g/12 oz potatoes
- 1–2 garlic cloves, crushed
- 4 spring onions, chopped
- 55 g/2 oz sweetcorn kernels
- vegetable oil, for shallow-frying

onion & tomato relish

- 1 onion
- 225 g/8 oz tomatoes
- 2 tbsp chopped fresh coriander
- 2 tbsp chopped fresh mint
- 2 tbsp lemon juice
- ½ tsp roasted cumin seeds
- ¼ tsp salt
- pinch of cayenne pepper

1 First make the relish. Cut the onion and tomatoes into small dice and place in a bowl with the remaining ingredients. Mix together well and leave to stand for at least 15 minutes before serving to allow the flavours to blend.

2 Place the flour in a bowl, stir in the spices and salt and make a well in the centre. Add the egg and milk and mix to form a fairly thick batter.

3 Coarsely grate the potatoes, place them in a sieve and rinse well under cold running water. Drain and squeeze dry, then stir them into the batter with the garlic, spring onions and sweetcorn and mix to combine thoroughly.

4 Heat about 5 mm/¼ inch of oil in a large frying pan and add a few tablespoons of the mixture at a time, flattening each to form a thin cake. Fry over a low heat, turning frequently, for 2–3 minutes, or until golden brown and cooked through.

5 Drain the fritters on kitchen paper and keep them hot while frying the remaining mixture in the same way. Serve the potato fritters hot with the relish.

Celeriac Soup with Cheese Pastry Sticks

Serves 4

ingredients
- 3 tbsp olive oil
- 1 onion, chopped
- 1 celeriac, peeled and cut into chunks
- 1 litre/1¾ pints vegetable stock
- 1 small bunch of fresh thyme, chopped, plus extra sprigs to garnish
- salt and pepper

cheese pastry sticks
- butter, for greasing
- 375 g/13 oz ready-made puff pastry, thawed if frozen
- plain flour, for dusting
- 1 egg, beaten
- 100 g/3½ oz Parmesan cheese, finely grated
- pepper

1 Heat the oil in a large saucepan over a medium heat, add the onion and cook, stirring frequently, for 4–5 minutes, until softened but not coloured. Add the celeriac and cook, stirring frequently, for 3–4 minutes. Pour in the stock and add the chopped thyme. Simmer for 25 minutes, or until the celeriac is tender.

2 Meanwhile, preheat the oven to 200°C/400°F/Gas Mark 6. Lightly grease two baking trays.

3 For the pastry sticks, roll the pastry out thinly on a floured work surface. Brush with half the egg and scatter over half the Parmesan cheese. Add a good grinding of pepper. Fold the pastry in half. Brush with the remaining egg, scatter with the remaining cheese and add another grinding of pepper. Cut into strips measuring about 1 cm/½ inch wide. Twist the pastry strips gently along their length to produce spiral shapes.

4 Place the pastry strips onto the prepared baking trays. Bake in the preheated oven for 5 minutes, or until crisp and golden.

5 Transfer the soup to a blender, in batches if necessary, and process until smooth. Alternatively, use a hand-held blender to process the soup until smooth in the saucepan. Gently reheat the soup in the saucepan. Season to taste with salt and pepper.

6 Ladle the soup into warmed bowls and garnish with thyme sprigs. Serve with the warm pastry sticks.

Carrot & Orange Stir-fry

Serves 4

ingredients

- 2 tbsp sunflower oil
- 450 g/1 lb carrots, grated
- 225 g/8 oz leeks, shredded
- 2 oranges, peeled and segmented
- 2 tbsp tomato ketchup
- 1 tbsp demerara sugar
- 2 tbsp light soy sauce
- 100 g/3½ oz peanuts, chopped

1 Heat the oil in a large wok. Add the carrots and leeks to the wok and stir-fry for 2–3 minutes, or until the vegetables are just soft.

2 Add the oranges to the wok and heat through gently, ensuring that you do not break up the orange segments as you stir the mixture.

3 Mix the ketchup, sugar and soy sauce together in a small bowl.

4 Add the ketchup mixture to the wok and stir-fry for a further 2 minutes.

5 Transfer the stir-fry to warmed serving bowls and scatter over the peanuts. Serve immediately.

Carrot Tarte Tatin

Serves 4

ingredients
- 600 g/1 lb 5 oz young carrots, cut into 2.5-cm/1-inch chunks
- 2 tbsp runny honey
- 50 g/1¾ oz butter
- 1 small bunch of fresh thyme, chopped
- 350 g/12 oz ready-made puff pastry, thawed if frozen
- plain flour, for dusting
- salt and pepper

1 Preheat the oven to 200°C/400°F/ Gas Mark 6.

2 Cook the carrots in a saucepan of boiling water for 10–15 minutes, until just tender. Drain, toss with the honey, butter and thyme, and season to taste with salt and pepper. Spoon over the base of a 20-cm/8-inch tarte tatin tin or round cake tin with a depth of about 3 cm/1¼ inches and roast in the preheated oven for 15 minutes, or until the carrots are caramelized.

3 Roll the pastry out on a floured work surface into a round large enough to fit the tin and give a 2-cm/¾-inch overlap. Lay the pastry carefully over the carrots and tuck the edges down between the carrots and the side of the tin to make a border. Bake in the oven for 15 minutes, or until the pastry is puffed and golden.

4 Remove the tin from the oven and turn out onto a plate. Serve immediately.

Roasted Root Vegetables

Serves 4–6

ingredients

- 3 parsnips, cut into 5-cm/2-inch chunks
- 4 baby turnips, cut into quarters
- 3 carrots, cut into 5-cm/2-inch chunks
- 450 g/1 lb butternut squash, peeled and cut into 5-cm/2-inch chunks
- 450 g/1 lb sweet potatoes, peeled and cut into 5-cm/2-inch chunks
- 2 garlic cloves, finely chopped
- 2 tbsp chopped fresh rosemary
- 2 tbsp chopped fresh thyme
- 2 tsp chopped fresh sage
- 3 tbsp olive oil
- salt and pepper
- 2 tbsp chopped fresh mixed herbs, such as parsley, thyme and mint, to garnish

1 Preheat the oven to 220ºC/425ºF/ Gas Mark 7.

2 Arrange all the vegetables in a single layer in a large roasting tin. Scatter over the garlic, rosemary, thyme and sage. Pour over the oil and season well with salt and pepper.

3 Toss all the ingredients together until they are well mixed and coated with the oil (you can leave them to marinate at this stage to allow the flavours to be absorbed).

4 Roast the vegetables at the top of the preheated oven for 50–60 minutes, until they are cooked and nicely browned. Turn the vegetables over halfway through the cooking time. Serve immediately, garnished with the mixed herbs.

Chapter 3
Brassicas & Salad Leaves

Directory of Brassicas & Salad Leaves

This varied group includes leafy greens, such as spinach and kale, as well as the more exotic pak choi. Brassicas also includes cabbage and Brussels sprouts, flowering vegetables, such as broccoli and cauliflower, and a tasty range of salad leaves.

Broccoli

There are two types of broccoli: the sprouting type and calabrese. Sprouting broccoli has long leafy stems and small purple or cream flower heads. Calabrese has a broad, tightly budded head divided into florets, and a thick central stalk. Thinly sliced, the stalk can be lightly steamed with the florets or served raw as a crudité.

Brussels sprouts

Reminiscent of Christmas, Brussels sprouts are like miniature cabbages and have a strong, nutty flavour. They are best cooked very lightly, either steamed or stir-fried.

Cabbage

When lightly cooked or served shredded in a salad, cabbage is delicious. Varieties range from the crinkly-leaved Savoy, which is ideal for stuffing, to the smooth, firm, white and red varieties. Chinese cabbage has a more delicate flavour and is best used in salads or stir-fries.

Cauliflower

Cauliflower comes in many varieties, ranging from white to pale green and purple. Cauliflower is cooked in the same way as calabrese. It has an understated flavour, which is enhanced by creamy sauces or melted cheese. It is also good in curries.

Chard and spinach beet

Chard has dark green, crinkled leaves and a broad white, yellow, pink or red stem. The stem takes longer to cook than the leaves, so it is best sliced and cooked slightly before the leaves are added. Spinach beet is similar to Swiss chard, but with narrower stems and a milder flavour.

Chicory and radicchio

The elongated, tightly packed leaves of red or white chicory, and the firm, round heads of radicchio have a slightly bitter taste, so use sparingly in salads. Both are good grilled, sautéed or braised, which mellow the flavour.

Endives

There are two basic types of endive: escarole or batavia with broad creased leaves, and curly endive or frisée with frilly leaves. The flavour is mild with only a hint of bitterness.

Kale and spring greens

Kale has curly-edged, long-stemmed leaves attached to a central stalk. Spring greens are similar but with larger, smoother leaves. Both are full of flavour and packed with nutrients. They are best steamed or lightly boiled. The young leaves can be used in stir-fries or raw in salads.

Lettuce

Cos and Webbs have firm, crisp leaves, while Little Gem is softer and sweeter. The pretty frilly leaves of Lollo Rosso are green at the base and a deep red around the edge. Equally attractive is the dark red oakleaf lettuce. Lettuces are very good braised or turned into flavoursome soups.

Pak choi

Pak choi has densely packed, dark green leaves with a white, fleshy base. It has a mild flavour, and makes a delightful addition to stir-fries, soups, noodle dishes and salads. For stir-frying it's best to cut the green leafy part from the base as the base takes longer to cook.

Rocket and watercress

Rocket and watercress have a distinctive, peppery flavour and will enliven any salad. They are milder when cooked, though still retaining some bite. They make delicious soups and sauces, and can be stirred into pasta or risotto.

Spinach

One of the most versatile leafy greens, spinach has a rich, buttery flavour and smooth texture. It's best either lightly boiled or steamed, or quickly sautéed in butter. Spinach is also good added to a risotto or pasta dish. Eaten raw, the young leaves make a highly nutritious addition to a salad.

Broccoli & Cheddar Soup

Serves 6

ingredients
- 25 g/1 oz butter
- 1 onion, chopped
- 2 tsp chopped fresh tarragon, plus extra to garnish
- 450 g/1 lb potatoes, grated
- 1.7 litres/3 pints vegetable stock
- 700 g/1 lb 9 oz broccoli, cut into small florets
- 175 g/6 oz Cheddar cheese, grated
- 1 tbsp chopped fresh parsley
- salt and pepper

1 Melt the butter in a large heavy-based saucepan. Add the onion and cook, stirring occasionally, for 5 minutes, until soft. Add the tarragon to the saucepan with the potatoes, season to taste with salt and pepper and mix well. Pour in just enough of the stock to cover and bring to the boil. Reduce the heat, cover and simmer for 10 minutes.

2 Meanwhile, bring the remaining stock to the boil in a separate saucepan. Add the broccoli and cook for 6–8 minutes, until just tender.

3 Remove both pans from the heat, leave to cool slightly, then ladle the contents of both into a blender or food processor, in batches if necessary. Process until smooth, then pour the mixture into a clean saucepan.

4 Stir the cheese into the pan with the parsley and heat gently to warm through, but do not allow the soup to boil. Ladle into warmed soup bowls, garnish with tarragon and serve immediately.

Broccoli & Wild Garlic
Crostini

Serves 6

ingredients
- 500 g/1 lb 2 oz broccoli, cut into small florets
- 100 ml/3½ fl oz olive oil
- 1 small bunch of wild garlic, rinsed, patted dry and chopped
- 1–2 fresh red chillies, deseeded and finely chopped
- 6 slices of country-style bread
- salt and pepper

1 Preheat the oven to 190°C/375°F/ Gas Mark 5.

2 Cook the broccoli in a large saucepan of boiling salted water for 10 minutes, or until just tender. Drain well and set aside.

3 Heat about one third of the oil in a wok or large frying pan over a high heat, add the wild garlic and chilli and stir-fry for 2 minutes. Add the broccoli, season to taste with salt and pepper and stir-fry for 3–4 minutes, until hot and crisp.

4 Meanwhile, drizzle the remaining oil evenly over the bread slices and bake in the preheated oven for 10 minutes, or until crisp and golden.

5 Divide the broccoli mixture among the crostini, season to taste with pepper and serve immediately.

Chilli Broccoli Pasta

Serves 4

ingredients
- 225 g/8 oz dried tortiglioni
- 225 g/8 oz broccoli
- 50 ml/2 fl oz extra virgin olive oil
- 2 large garlic cloves, chopped
- 2 fresh red chillies, deseeded and diced
- 8 cherry tomatoes, halved if large (optional)
- salt
- small handful of chopped fresh basil or parsley, to garnish

1 Bring a large saucepan of lightly salted water to the boil. Add the pasta, return to the boil and cook for 8–10 minutes, until the pasta is tender but still firm to the bite. Remove from the heat, drain, rinse with cold water and drain again. Set aside.

2 Cut the broccoli into florets. Bring a saucepan of lightly salted water to the boil, add the broccoli and cook for 5 minutes. Drain, rinse with cold water and drain again.

3 Heat the oil in the pan that the pasta was cooked in. Add the garlic, chillies and tomatoes, if using. Cook over a high heat for 1 minute.

4 Return the broccoli to the pan and mix well. Cook for 2 minutes to heat through. Add the pasta and mix well again. Cook for a further minute.

5 Remove the pasta from the heat, tip into a large serving bowl and serve, garnished with basil.

Cauliflower & Broccoli Flan

Serves 4

ingredients

pastry
- 175 g/6 oz plain flour, plus extra for dusting
- pinch of salt
- 1¼ tsp paprika
- 1 tsp dried thyme
- 75 g/2¾ oz margarine
- 3 tbsp water

filling
- 100 g/3½ oz cauliflower florets
- 100 g/3½ oz broccoli florets
- 1 onion, cut into 8 wedges
- 25 g/1 oz butter or margarine
- 1 tbsp plain flour
- 6 tbsp vegetable stock
- 125 ml/4 fl oz milk
- 85 g/3 oz Cheddar cheese, grated
- salt and pepper
- paprika, to garnish

1 Preheat the oven to 190°C/375°F/ Gas Mark 5. To make the pastry, sift the flour and salt into a bowl. Add the paprika and thyme and rub in the margarine. Stir in the water and bind to form a dough. Leave to chill in the refrigerator for 30 minutes.

2 Roll out the pastry on a floured work surface and use to line an 18-cm/ 7-inch loose-based flan tin. Prick the base with a fork and line with baking paper. Fill with baking beans and bake in the preheated oven for 15 minutes. Remove the paper and beans and return the pastry case to the oven for 5 minutes.

3 To make the filling, bring a large saucepan of lightly salted water to the boil, add the cauliflower, broccoli and onion and cook for 10–12 minutes, until tender. Drain and reserve.

4 Melt the butter in a saucepan. Add the flour and cook, stirring constantly, for 1 minute. Remove from the heat, stir in the stock and milk and return to the heat. Bring to the boil, stirring constantly, and add 55 g/2 oz of the cheese. Season to taste with salt and pepper.

5 Spoon the cauliflower, broccoli and onion into the pastry case. Pour over the sauce and sprinkle with the remaining cheese. Return the flan to the oven and bake for 10 minutes, until the cheese is golden and bubbling. Garnish with paprika and serve immediately.

Cauliflower, Aubergine & Green Bean Korma

Serves 4–6

ingredients

- 85 g/3 oz cashew nuts
- 1½ tbsp garlic and ginger paste
- 200 ml/7 fl oz water, plus extra if needed
- 55 g/2 oz ghee or 4 tbsp vegetable or groundnut oil
- 1 large onion, chopped
- 5 green cardamom pods, lightly crushed
- 1 cinnamon stick, broken in half
- ¼ tsp ground turmeric
- 250 ml/9 fl oz double cream
- 140 g/5 oz new potatoes, scrubbed and chopped into 1-cm/½-inch pieces
- 140 g/5 oz cauliflower florets
- ½ tsp garam masala
- 140 g/5 oz aubergine, cut into chunks
- 140 g/5 oz green beans, cut into 1-cm/½-inch lengths
- salt and pepper
- chopped fresh mint or coriander, to garnish

1 Heat a large flameproof casserole or frying pan with a tight-fitting lid over a high heat. Add the nuts and stir until they start to brown, then tip them out of the casserole.

2 Put the nuts in a spice blender with the garlic and ginger paste and 1 tablespoon of the water and process until a coarse paste forms.

3 Melt the ghee in the casserole over a medium–high heat. Add the onion and fry for 5–8 minutes, or until golden brown. Add the nut paste and stir for 5 minutes. Stir in the cardamom pods, cinnamon stick and turmeric. Add the cream and the remaining water and bring to the boil, stirring. Reduce the heat to the lowest level, cover the casserole and simmer for 5 minutes.

4 Add the potatoes, cauliflower and garam masala to the casserole and simmer, covered, for 5 minutes. Stir in the aubergine and green beans and continue simmering for a further 5 minutes, or until all the vegetables are tender. Check the sauce occasionally to make sure it isn't sticking to the base of the casserole, and stir in extra water if needed.

5 Taste and adjust the seasoning, adding salt and pepper if needed. Sprinkle with mint and serve.

Cauliflower Cheese

Serves 4

ingredients

- 1 cauliflower, trimmed and cut into florets (675 g/1 lb 8 oz prepared weight)
- 40 g/1½ oz butter
- 40 g/1½ oz plain flour
- 450 ml/16 fl oz milk
- 115 g/4 oz Cheddar cheese, finely grated
- freshly grated nutmeg
- salt and pepper
- 1 tbsp grated Parmesan cheese

1 Preheat the grill to high. Cook the cauliflower in a saucepan of boiling salted water for 4–5 minutes. It should still be firm. Drain, place in a hot 1.4-litre/2½-pint gratin dish and keep warm.

2 Melt the butter in the rinsed-out saucepan over a medium heat and stir in the flour. Cook, stirring continuously, for 1 minute, until smooth.

3 Remove from the heat and gradually stir in the milk until you have a smooth consistency.

4 Return to a low heat and continue to stir while the sauce comes to the boil and thickens. Reduce the heat and simmer gently, stirring constantly, for about 3 minutes, until the sauce is creamy and smooth.

5 Remove from the heat and stir in the Cheddar cheese and nutmeg to taste. Taste and season well with salt and pepper.

6 Pour the hot sauce over the cauliflower, top with the Parmesan and place under the preheated grill to brown. Serve immediately.

Brussels Sprouts
with Chestnuts

Serves 4

ingredients
- 450 g/1 lb Brussels sprouts
- 115 g/4 oz unsalted butter
- 55 g/2 oz brown sugar
- 115 g/4 oz cooked and shelled chestnuts
- salt and pepper

1 Trim the sprouts, removing the coarse stems and any loose outer leaves. Bring a large saucepan of lightly salted water to the boil over a high heat. Add the sprouts and boil for 5–10 minutes, until just cooked but not too soft. Drain well, rinse in cold water and drain again. Set aside.

2 Melt the butter in a heavy-based frying pan. Add the sugar and stir over a medium heat until dissolved.

3 Add the chestnuts to the pan and cook, stirring occasionally, until they are well coated and starting to brown.

4 Add the sprouts to the pan with the chestnuts and mix well. Reduce the heat and cook gently, stirring occasionally, for 3–4 minutes to heat through. Season to taste with salt and pepper.

5 Remove from the heat, transfer to a serving dish and serve.

Traditional Tuscan
Bean & Cabbage Soup

Serves 6

ingredients
- 200 g/7 oz dried cannellini beans, soaked in cold water overnight
- 3 tbsp olive oil
- 2 red onions, roughly chopped
- 4 carrots, sliced
- 4 celery sticks, roughly chopped
- 4 garlic cloves, roughly chopped
- 600 ml/1 pint water or vegetable stock
- 400 g/14 oz canned chopped tomatoes
- 2 tbsp chopped fresh flat-leaf parsley
- 500 g/1 lb 2 oz cavolo nero, trimmed and finely sliced
- 1 small 2-day-old ciabatta loaf, torn into small pieces
- salt and pepper
- extra virgin olive oil, to serve

1 Drain the beans and put in a large saucepan. Cover with fresh cold water and bring to the boil, skimming off any foam that rises to the surface. Reduce the heat and simmer, uncovered, for 1–1½ hours, until tender, topping up with water if required.

2 Meanwhile, heat the olive oil in a large saucepan, add the onions, carrots and celery and cook over a medium heat, stirring frequently, for 10–15 minutes, until soft. Add the garlic and cook, stirring, for 1–2 minutes.

3 Drain the beans, reserving the cooking water, and add half the beans to the vegetable mixture. Pour in the measured water and the tomatoes, add the parsley and season well with salt and pepper. Bring to a simmer and cook, uncovered and stirring occasionally, for 30 minutes. Add the cavolo nero and cook, stirring occasionally, for a further 15 minutes.

4 Put the remaining beans in a food processor or blender with some of the reserved cooking water and process until smooth. Add to the soup. Stir in the bread. The soup should be thick, but add more of the reserved cooking water to thin if necessary. Continue to cook until heated through.

5 Serve hot, drizzled with extra virgin olive oil.

Kale Stir-fry

Serves 4

ingredients
- 750 g/1 lb 10 oz kale
- 2 tbsp sunflower oil
- 1 onion, chopped
- 4 large garlic cloves, finely chopped
- 2 red peppers, deseeded and thinly sliced
- 1 large carrot, coarsely grated
- 100 g/3½ oz broccoli, cut into very small florets
- pinch of dried chilli flakes (optional)
- 125 ml/4 fl oz vegetable stock
- 115 g/4 oz mixed sprouted beans
- handful of toasted cashew nuts, chopped
- salt and pepper
- lemon wedges, to serve

1 Using a sharp knife, cut out the thick central stems from the kale. Stack several leaves on top of each other, then cut across them to finely shred; repeat until all the kale is shredded. Set aside.

2 Heat a large wok with a lid over a high heat until a splash of water 'dances' on the surface. Add the oil and swirl it around. Add the onion and stir-fry for about 3 minutes, then add the garlic, peppers and carrot and continue stir-frying until the onion is tender and the peppers are starting to soften.

3 Add the broccoli and chilli flakes, if using, and stir. Add the kale to the wok and stir. Add the stock and salt and pepper to taste, reduce the heat to medium, cover the wok and simmer for about 5 minutes, until the kale is tender.

4 Remove the lid and allow any excess liquid to evaporate. Use 2 forks to mix the sprouted beans through the other ingredients, then adjust the seasoning, adding salt and pepper if needed.

5 Transfer to serving plates, scatter over the nuts and serve with lemon wedges.

Stuffed Cabbage Rolls

Serves 4

ingredients

- 8 large or 12 medium green cabbage leaves
- 1 litre/1¾ pints water
- 100 g/3½ oz pearl barley, rinsed and drained
- 2 tbsp chopped fresh parsley
- 2 garlic cloves, roughly chopped
- 800 g/1 lb 12 oz canned chopped tomatoes
- 4 tbsp red wine vinegar
- 1 tbsp sunflower or corn oil, plus extra for brushing
- 2 courgettes, diced
- 3 spring onions, sliced
- 2 tbsp brown sugar
- salt and pepper

1 Cut out the thick central stems from the cabbage leaves. Bring a large saucepan of water to the boil, add the cabbage leaves and blanch for 1 minute. Drain the leaves well and spread out to dry.

2 Bring the measured water to the boil in a large saucepan. Add the barley and half the chopped parsley, cover and simmer for about 45 minutes, until the liquid has been absorbed.

3 Meanwhile, put the garlic, half the tomatoes and the vinegar in a blender or food processor and process to a smooth purée. Scrape into a bowl and set aside.

4 Heat the oil in a large frying pan. Add the courgettes and the remaining parsley and cook, stirring frequently, for 3 minutes. Add the spring onions and cook briefly, then add the tomato mixture. Cook for about 10 minutes, until thickened, then transfer to a large bowl.

5 Add the cooked barley to the bowl, season to taste with salt and pepper and stir well.

6 Preheat the oven to 190°C/375°F/Gas Mark 5. Lightly brush an ovenproof dish with oil. Place a spoonful of the barley mixture at the stem end of a cabbage leaf. Roll up, tucking in the sides, and place, seam-side down, in the dish. Stuff and roll the remaining cabbage leaves in the same way, placing them in the dish in a single layer.

7 Sprinkle the sugar over the cabbage rolls and pour the remaining tomatoes, with their can juices, on top. Cover with foil and bake in the preheated oven for 30 minutes, or until tender. Serve straight from the dish.

Red Curry with Mixed Leaves

Serves 4

ingredients
- 2 tbsp groundnut or vegetable oil
- 2 onions, thinly sliced
- 1 bunch of fine asparagus spears
- 400 ml/14 fl oz canned coconut milk
- 2 tbsp Thai red curry paste
- 3 fresh kaffir lime leaves
- 225 g/8 oz baby spinach leaves
- 2 heads of pak choi, chopped
- 1 small head of Chinese leaves, shredded
- handful of fresh coriander, chopped
- cooked rice, to serve

1 Heat the oil in a wok, add the onions and asparagus and stir-fry over a medium–high heat for 1–2 minutes.

2 Add the coconut milk, curry paste and lime leaves and bring gently to the boil, stirring occasionally.

3 Add the spinach, pak choi and Chinese leaves and cook, stirring, for 2–3 minutes, until wilted.

4 Add the coriander and stir well. Serve immediately with rice.

Spinach & Ricotta Gnocchi

Serves 4–6

ingredients
- 1 tbsp olive oil
- 500 g/1 lb 2 oz spinach leaves
- 225 g/8 oz ricotta cheese
- 115 g/4 oz Parmesan or pecorino cheese, grated
- 2 eggs, lightly beaten
- 55 g/2 oz plain flour, plus extra for dusting
- freshly grated nutmeg
- salt and pepper
- fresh basil leaves, shredded, to garnish

sauce
- 2 tbsp olive oil
- 2 shallots, finely chopped
- 1 carrot, finely diced
- 2 garlic cloves, crushed
- 800 g/1 lb 12 oz canned chopped tomatoes
- 1 tbsp tomato purée
- 6 fresh basil leaves, roughly torn into pieces
- salt and pepper

1 Heat the oil in a large saucepan. Add the spinach and cook, covered, for 1–2 minutes, until just wilted. Drain through a sieve and leave to cool, then squeeze out as much water as possible with your hands (you can squeeze it in a clean tea towel to ensure that it is very dry).

2 Finely chop the spinach and put in a bowl. Add the ricotta cheese, half the Parmesan cheese, the eggs and flour and mix well. Season to taste with salt, pepper and nutmeg. Cover and chill in the refrigerator for at least 1 hour.

3 Meanwhile, make the sauce. Heat the oil in a saucepan, add the shallots, carrot and garlic and cook over a medium heat, stirring frequently, for 3–4 minutes, until soft. Add the tomatoes and tomato purée and bring to the boil, then reduce the heat and simmer, uncovered, for 10–15 minutes, until the sauce is reduced and thickened. Season to taste with salt and pepper and add the basil leaves. If you like a smooth sauce, pass it through a sieve or process in a food processor or blender.

4 To shape the gnocchi, flour a plate and your hands thoroughly. Put a dessertspoonful of the spinach mixture into the palm of one hand, roll gently into an egg shape and transfer to a floured baking tray. Repeat with the remaining spinach mixture.

5 Bring a large saucepan of water to a simmer, carefully add the gnocchi, in small batches, and cook gently for 2–3 minutes, until they rise to the surface. Remove with a slotted spoon and transfer to a warmed dish to keep warm while you cook the remaining gnocchi.

6 Transfer the gnocchi to individual serving dishes and pour over the sauce. Garnish with basil and serve immediately with the remaining Parmesan cheese.

Pasta with Honeyed
Chicory & Toasted Walnuts

Serves 4

ingredients

- 3 tbsp olive oil
- 2 garlic cloves, crushed
- 3 heads of chicory, sliced
- 1 tbsp runny honey
- 100 g/3½ oz walnuts
- 450 g/1 lb dried penne
- salt and pepper

1 Heat the oil in a frying pan over a low heat, add the garlic and chicory and cook, stirring, for 3–4 minutes, until the chicory begins to wilt. Stir in the honey and walnuts and cook, stirring occasionally, for a further 4–5 minutes. Season to taste with salt and pepper.

2 Meanwhile, bring a large saucepan of lightly salted water to the boil. Add the pasta, return to the boil and cook for 8–10 minutes, or until the pasta is tender but still firm to the bite.

3 Drain the pasta and toss with the chicory mixture. Serve immediately.

Watercress, Courgette & Mint Salad

Serves 4

ingredients

- 2 courgettes, cut into batons
- 100 g/3½ oz green beans, cut into short lengths
- 1 green pepper, deseeded and cut into strips
- 2 celery sticks, sliced
- 1 bunch of watercress
- salt

dressing

- 200 ml/7 fl oz natural yogurt
- 1 garlic clove, crushed
- 2 tbsp chopped fresh mint
- pepper

1 Bring a saucepan of lightly salted water to the boil, add the courgettes and beans and cook for 7–8 minutes. Drain, rinse under cold running water and drain again. Set aside to cool completely.

2 Mix the courgettes and beans with the green pepper, celery and watercress in a large serving bowl.

3 To make the dressing, combine the yogurt, garlic and mint in a small bowl. Season to taste with pepper.

4 Spoon the dressing onto the salad and serve immediately.

Spaghetti with Rocket &
Hazelnut Pesto

Serves 4

ingredients

- 2 garlic cloves
- 85 g/3 oz hazelnuts
- 150 g/5½ oz rocket, coarse stalks removed
- 115 g/4 oz Parmesan cheese, grated, plus extra to serve
- 6 tbsp extra virgin olive oil
- 115 g/4 oz mascarpone cheese
- 400 g/14 oz dried spaghetti
- salt and pepper

1 Put the garlic and hazelnuts in a food processor and process until finely chopped. Add the rocket, Parmesan and oil and process until smooth and thoroughly combined. Scrape the pesto into a large serving dish, season to taste with salt and pepper and stir in the mascarpone.

2 Bring a large saucepan of salted water to the boil. Add the pasta, return to the boil and cook for 8–10 minutes, until tender but still firm to the bite.

3 Stir 100–150 ml/3½–5 fl oz of the pasta cooking water into the pesto, mixing well until thoroughly combined. Drain the pasta, add it to the dish and toss well to coat. Sprinkle with Parmesan and serve immediately.

Radicchio & Red Pepper Salad

Serves 4

ingredients
- 2 red peppers
- 1 head of radicchio, separated into leaves
- 4 cooked whole beetroots, cut into matchsticks
- 12 radishes, sliced
- 4 spring onions, finely chopped
- 4 tbsp ready-made salad dressing
- crusty bread, to serve

1 Core and deseed the red peppers and cut into rounds.

2 Arrange the radicchio leaves in a salad bowl. Add the peppers, beetroots, radishes and spring onions.

3 Drizzle with the dressing, toss well and serve with crusty bread.

Chapter 4
Mushrooms &
the Onion Family

Directory of Mushrooms & the Onion Family

Both mushrooms and the onion family have traditionally been used to provide the base for many dishes, although, as this chapter shows, they really come into their own when served as the star of many delicious main-course dishes.

Mushrooms

There is a wide range of mushrooms from which to choose, both fresh and dried, and many types of wild mushroom are now cultivated. They are extremely versatile and can be eaten raw in salads, cooked as a vegetable accompaniment or used to flavour a variety of dishes ranging from soups to risottos.

Dried mushrooms keep well: to reconstitute them, soak in boiling water for 20–30 minutes. Drain and rinse well to remove any dirt and grit. Use the soaking water in stocks and sauces, but strain first.

Ceps

Also known as the 'penny bun', ceps have a meaty texture and woody flavour. Dried ceps lend a rich flavour to soups, stocks and sauces.

Chanterelles

Highly prized, golden-coloured chanterelles have a fruity, nutty flavour. They should be wiped rather than washed, as they are very porous. Most types of mushroom should be prepared in this way, apart from the honeycomb-capped morel.

Chestnut

Chestnut mushrooms are medium-sized with a closed cup and brown skin. They have a richer flavour than the white variety.

Cremini and portabellos

Creminis are intensely flavoured, brown button mushrooms. They are a miniature version of the portabello – a large, flat, dense-fleshed mushroom with a meaty flavour.

Morels

Instantly recognizable by the cone-shaped honeycomb cap, morels are a rare variety of mushroom appearing only in the spring. They have an open, porous texture and a mild, sweetish flavour. Dried morels are also available.

Shiitake and oyster

Both shiitake and oyster mushrooms are now widely cultivated. Oysters are fluted in shape, and while they are usually greyish-brown in colour, they also come in pale yellow and pink. The flavour is mild. Shiitakes have a chewy texture and robust flavour, and are most commonly used in Asian dishes.

Onion family

Garlic, leeks, onions and shallots provide substance and unifying flavour to all manner of savoury dishes, particularly those for vegetarians. They are also delicious cooked on their own.

Garlic

Amazingly versatile, garlic adds essential flavour to dishes from all over the world. Whole heads of garlic are also delicious roasted and served as a vegetable. Used raw, the crushed cloves can be mashed with butter for garnishing grilled meat, or added to mayonnaise to make aïoli.

Leeks

Leeks taste better lightly steamed or sautéed rather than boiled, which can make them soggy. They are a key ingredient in hearty soups, and also combine well with eggs and cream in savoury tarts. Baby leeks are delicious quickly roasted in a very hot oven. They can also be sliced paper-thin and added sparingly to salads.

Onions

Onions offer a range of taste sensations from the sweet and mild Spanish onion and light, fresh-tasting spring onion to the versatile and pungent yellow onion. Once cooked, the flavour becomes mellow – roasting is a particularly good way of bringing out their delicious sweetness. Baby onions or pickling onions are good cooked whole in a stew or braised; they are also useful for kebabs. Red and white onions are delicious thinly sliced and scattered over salads.

Shallots

There are two types of shallot: the large single bulb torpedo variety, sometimes called a banana shallot, and the smaller round ones that divide into two cloves. Shallots have a distinctive sweet, piquant and full-bodied flavour that forms the base of many classic French sauces. Shallots also feature in Southeast Asian cuisine, where they are deep-fried and used as a crisp topping for salads and rice dishes.

Mushroom & Barley Soup

Serves 4

ingredients
- 55 g/2 oz pearl barley
- 1.5 litres/2¾ pints vegetable stock
- 1 bay leaf
- 15 g/½ oz butter
- 350 g/12 oz mushrooms, thinly sliced
- 1 tsp olive oil
- 1 onion, finely chopped
- 2 carrots, thinly sliced
- 1 tbsp chopped fresh tarragon, plus extra leaves to garnish
- 1 tbsp chopped fresh parsley, plus extra to garnish
- salt and pepper

1 Rinse the pearl barley and drain. Bring 450 ml/16 fl oz of the stock to the boil in a small saucepan. Add the bay leaf and, if the stock is unsalted, add a large pinch of salt. Stir in the pearl barley, reduce the heat, cover and simmer for 40 minutes.

2 Melt the butter in a large frying pan over a medium heat. Add the mushrooms and season to taste with salt and pepper. Cook, stirring occasionally at first and more often as the mushrooms start to colour, for 8 minutes, until they are golden brown. Remove from the heat.

3 Heat the oil in a large saucepan over a medium heat and add the onion and carrots. Cover and cook, stirring frequently, for 3 minutes, or until the onion is softened.

4 Add the remaining stock to the saucepan with the onion and carrots and bring to the boil. Stir in the pearl barley with its cooking liquid and add the mushrooms. Reduce the heat, cover and simmer gently, stirring occasionally, for about 20 minutes, or until the carrots are tender.

5 Stir in the chopped tarragon and parsley. Taste and adjust the seasoning, adding salt and pepper if needed. Ladle into warmed bowls, garnish with chopped parsley and tarragon leaves, and serve.

Mixed Mushroom Pizza

Makes 2

ingredients
- 3 tbsp oil
- 2 garlic cloves, crushed
- 2 tbsp chopped fresh oregano
- 2 x 23-cm/9-inch ready-made thin-and-crispy pizza bases
- 85 g/3 oz ricotta cheese
- 1 tbsp milk
- 40 g/1½ oz butter
- 350 g/12 oz mixed mushrooms, sliced
- 2 tsp lemon juice
- 1 tbsp chopped fresh marjoram
- 4 tbsp grated Parmesan cheese
- salt and pepper

1 Preheat the oven to 240°C/475°F/Gas Mark 9. Mix 2 tablespoons of the oil, the garlic and oregano together and brush over the pizza bases.

2 Mix the ricotta cheese and milk together in a bowl. Season to taste with salt and pepper and spread the mixture over the pizza bases, leaving a 4-cm/1½-inch border around the edges.

3 Heat the butter and the remaining oil together in a large frying pan. Add the mushrooms and cook over a high heat for 2 minutes. Remove the frying pan from the heat, season to taste with salt and pepper and stir in the lemon juice and marjoram.

4 Spoon the mushroom mixture over the pizza bases, leaving a 1-cm/½-inch border. Sprinkle with the Parmesan cheese, then bake in the preheated oven for 12–15 minutes, until the crusts are crisp and the mushrooms are cooked. Serve immediately.

Linguine with Mushroom &
Mascarpone Sauce

Serves 4

ingredients

- 450 g/1 lb dried linguine
- 55 g/2 oz butter
- 1 garlic clove, crushed
- 225 g/8 oz mixed wild
  mushrooms, sliced
- 250 g/9 oz mascarpone cheese
- 2 tbsp milk
- 1 tsp chopped fresh sage, plus
  extra leaves to garnish
- salt and pepper
- Parmesan cheese shavings,
  to serve

1 Bring a large saucepan of lightly salted water to the boil. Add the pasta, return to the boil and cook for 8–10 minutes, until tender but still firm to the bite.

2 Meanwhile, melt the butter in a separate large saucepan. Add the garlic and mushrooms and cook for 3–4 minutes. Reduce the heat and stir in the mascarpone cheese, milk and chopped sage. Season to taste with salt and pepper.

3 Drain the pasta thoroughly and add to the mushroom sauce. Toss until the pasta is well coated with the sauce. Transfer to warmed dishes, garnish with sage leaves and serve immediately with Parmesan cheese shavings.

Wild Mushroom Bruschetta

Serves 4

ingredients

- 4 slices of sourdough bread, such as Pugliese
- 3 garlic cloves, 1 halved and 2 crushed
- 2 tbsp extra virgin olive oil, plus extra for drizzling
- 225 g/8 oz mixed wild mushrooms, such as ceps, chanterelles and field mushrooms
- 1 tbsp olive oil
- 25 g/1 oz butter
- 1 small onion or 2 shallots, finely chopped
- 50 ml/2 fl oz dry white wine or Marsala
- salt and pepper
- 2 tbsp roughly chopped fresh flat-leaf parsley, to garnish

1 Preheat the grill to medium. Toast the bread slices on both sides under the preheated grill, rub with the garlic halves and drizzle with the extra virgin olive oil. Transfer to a baking tray and keep warm.

2 Wipe the mushrooms thoroughly to remove any trace of soil and slice any large ones. Heat the olive oil with half the butter in a frying pan, add the mushrooms and cook over a medium heat, stirring frequently, for 3–4 minutes, until soft. Remove with a slotted spoon and keep warm.

3 Heat the remaining butter in the frying pan, add the onion and crushed garlic and cook over a medium heat, stirring frequently, for 3–4 minutes, until soft. Add the wine, stir well and leave to bubble for 2–3 minutes, until reduced and thickened. Return the mushrooms to the frying pan and heat through. The sauce should be thick enough to glaze the mushrooms. Season to taste with salt and pepper.

4 Pile the mushrooms on top of the toasted bread, scatter with the parsley and serve immediately, drizzled with extra virgin olive oil.

Wild Mushroom Omelette

Serves 2

ingredients

- 1 tsp extra virgin olive oil
- 1 small onion, cut into wedges
- 2–3 garlic cloves, crushed
- 85 g/3 oz mixed wild mushrooms, halved if large
- 85 g/3 oz closed-cup mushrooms, sliced
- 1 courgette, grated
- 2 eggs
- 2 egg whites
- 2 tbsp water
- 1 yellow pepper, deseeded and cut into strips
- 1 tbsp grated Parmesan cheese (optional)
- 1 tbsp shredded fresh basil
- pepper
- rocket, to garnish
- wholemeal bread, to serve

1 Heat the oil in a large non-stick frying pan. Add the onion and garlic, cover and cook, stirring occasionally, for 3 minutes. Add the mushrooms and cook for a further 4–5 minutes, or until the mushrooms have softened slightly. Add the courgette.

2 Beat together the whole eggs, egg whites and water with pepper to taste. Pour into the frying pan, increase the heat slightly and cook, drawing the egg into the centre of the pan from the edges with a fork or spatula.

3 When the omelette is set on the base, sprinkle over the yellow pepper, followed by the Parmesan cheese, if using, and basil. Cook for a further 3–4 minutes, or until set to personal preference.

4 Cut the omelette into wedges, garnish with rocket and serve with wholemeal bread.

Mushroom Risotto

Serves 4

ingredients
- 55 g/2 oz dried wild mushrooms
- 250 ml/9 fl oz warm water
- 700 ml/1¼ pints vegetable stock
- 6 tbsp olive oil
- 280 g/10 oz mixed fresh wild or field mushrooms, thickly sliced
- 2 garlic cloves, finely chopped
- 1 tbsp finely chopped fresh thyme
- 1 onion, finely chopped
- 350 g/12 oz risotto rice
- 150 ml/5 fl oz dry white wine
- 55 g/2 oz butter
- 115 g/4 oz Parmesan cheese, grated
- salt and pepper
- 2 tbsp finely chopped fresh flat-leaf parsley, to garnish

1 Soak the dried mushrooms in the warm water in a small bowl for 10–15 minutes. Drain, reserving the soaking liquid (sieve it thoroughly to remove any grit). Finely slice the drained mushrooms.

2 Bring the stock to the boil, then reduce the heat and keep simmering gently over a low heat while you are cooking the risotto.

3 Heat half the oil in a deep frying pan, add the fresh mushrooms and cook over a low heat, stirring occasionally, for 10–15 minutes, until soft. Add the dried mushrooms and garlic and cook, stirring frequently, for a further 2–3 minutes. Add the thyme and salt and pepper to taste, then remove the mushroom mixture from the frying pan and keep warm.

4 Meanwhile, heat the remaining oil in the saucepan, add the onion and cook over a low heat, stirring occasionally, for 10–12 minutes, until soft. Gently stir in the rice and cook, stirring, for 1 minute, until the rice is translucent and coated with the oil.

5 Pour in the wine and cook, stirring, until it has all been absorbed. Add the reserved soaking liquid and cook, stirring, until it has all been absorbed.

6 Gradually add the hot stock, a ladleful at a time, stirring constantly. Add more stock as the rice absorbs each addition. Increase the heat so the liquid bubbles. Cook for 20–25 minutes, or until all the liquid has been absorbed and the rice is creamy but still firm to the bite.

7 Remove from the heat and gently stir in the mushroom mixture, butter and half the Parmesan cheese. Season to taste with salt and pepper.

8 Serve immediately on warmed plates, scattered with the parsley and the remaining Parmesan cheese.

Creamy Stuffed Mushrooms

Serves 4

ingredients
- 25 g/1 oz dried ceps
- 225 g/8 oz floury potatoes, diced
- 2 tbsp melted butter
- 4 tbsp double cream
- 2 tbsp snipped fresh chives
- 8 portobello mushrooms
- 25 g/1 oz Emmenthal cheese, grated
- 150 ml/5 fl oz vegetable stock
- salt and pepper

1 Preheat the oven to 220°C/425°F/Gas Mark 7. Place the dried ceps in a small bowl. Add enough boiling water to cover and leave to soak for 20 minutes.

2 Meanwhile, cook the potatoes in a saucepan of lightly salted boiling water for 10 minutes, until cooked through and tender. Drain well and mash until smooth.

3 Drain the soaked ceps and then chop them finely. Mix them into the mashed potatoes.

4 Thoroughly blend the butter, cream and chives together and pour into the potato mixture, mixing well. Season to taste with salt and pepper.

5 Remove the stalks from the portobello mushrooms. Chop the stalks and stir them into the potato mixture. Spoon the mixture into the mushrooms and sprinkle the cheese over the top.

6 Arrange the stuffed mushrooms in a shallow ovenproof dish and pour in the stock.

7 Cover the dish and cook in the preheated oven for 20 minutes. Uncover and cook for a further 5 minutes, until golden. Serve the mushrooms immediately.

Creamed Morels on
Spinach & Polenta Croûtons

Serves 6

ingredients
- 6 handfuls of fresh morels
- 3 tbsp olive oil
- 4 shallots, finely chopped
- 2 garlic cloves, crushed
- 100 ml/3½ fl oz Marsala
- 200 ml/7 fl oz double cream
- 2 tbsp wholegrain mustard
- 1 small bunch fresh tarragon, finely chopped, plus extra sprigs to garnish
- salt and pepper

polenta croûtons
- 1 litre/1¾ pints vegetable stock
- 250 g/9 oz polenta
- 100 g/3½ oz Parmesan cheese, grated
- 2 handfuls of baby spinach, roughly torn
- 2 tsp roughly cracked black peppercorns
- 100 g/3½ oz butter, softened
- salt and pepper
- olive oil, for oiling

1 To make the polenta croûtons, bring the stock to a rolling boil and add the polenta in a steady stream, stirring quickly with a large balloon whisk. Cook according to the packet instructions.

2 Using a wooden spoon, stir in the Parmesan cheese, spinach, peppercorns and half the butter. Taste and adjust the seasoning, adding salt and pepper if needed.

3 Lightly oil a baking tray. Pour the polenta mixture out onto the prepared baking tray, smooth over with a palette knife and leave to cool. When the polenta has set, use a 10-cm/4-inch round pastry cutter to cut out 6 rounds.

4 Cut the morels in half and gently wash them, taking care to remove any traces of soil and grit. Dry gently with kitchen paper.

5 Heat the oil in a saucepan over a medium heat, add the shallots and garlic and cook for 3–4 minutes, until softened. Add the morels and cook, stirring constantly, for 2 minutes. Pour in the Marsala and bubble briefly, then add the cream, mustard and chopped tarragon. Season to taste with salt and pepper. Keep warm.

6 Heat the remaining butter in a frying pan over a high heat, add the polenta croûtons and cook for 3–4 minutes on each side, until crisp and golden. Serve immediately, topped with the creamed morels and garnished with tarragon sprigs.

French Onion Soup

Serves 6

ingredients
- 3 tbsp olive oil
- 675 g/1 lb 8 oz onions, thinly sliced
- 4 garlic cloves, 3 chopped and 1 halved
- 1 tsp sugar
- 2 tsp chopped fresh thyme, plus extra sprigs to garnish
- 2 tbsp plain flour
- 125 ml/4 fl oz dry white wine
- 2 litres/3½ pints vegetable stock
- 6 slices of French bread
- 300 g/10½ oz Gruyère cheese, grated

1 Heat the oil in a large heavy-based saucepan, then add the onions and cook, stirring occasionally, for 10 minutes, until they are just beginning to brown. Stir in the chopped garlic, sugar and chopped thyme, then reduce the heat and cook, stirring occasionally, for 30 minutes, or until the onions are golden brown.

2 Sprinkle in the flour and cook, stirring, for 1–2 minutes. Stir in the wine. Gradually stir in the stock and bring to the boil, skimming off any foam that rises to the surface, then reduce the heat and simmer for 45 minutes.

3 Meanwhile, preheat the grill to medium. Toast the bread on both sides under the grill. Rub the toast with the garlic halves.

4 Ladle the soup into 6 flameproof bowls set on a baking tray. Float a piece of toast in each bowl and divide the cheese among them. Place under the preheated grill for 2–3 minutes, or until the cheese has just melted. Garnish with thyme sprigs and serve immediately.

Flatbread with Onion & Rosemary

Makes 1 loaf

ingredients
- 450 g/1 lb strong white flour, plus extra for dusting
- 1½ tsp easy-blend dried yeast
- ½ tsp salt
- 2 tbsp chopped fresh rosemary, plus extra small sprigs to garnish
- 5 tbsp extra virgin olive oil, plus extra for oiling
- 300 ml/10 fl oz warm water
- 1 red onion, finely sliced and separated into rings
- 1 tbsp sea salt

1 Mix the flour, yeast and salt together in a mixing bowl, then stir in the chopped rosemary. Make a well in the centre. Mix 3 tablespoons of the oil and the water together in a jug and pour into the well. Gradually mix the liquid into the flour mixture with a palette knife. Gather the mixture together with your hands to form a soft dough.

2 Turn out the dough onto a lightly floured work surface and knead for 8–10 minutes, until very smooth and elastic. Return the dough to the bowl, cover with a clean tea towel or oiled clingfilm and leave to rise in a warm place for 45 minutes –1 hour, or until doubled in size.

3 Preheat the oven to 200°C/400°F/ Gas Mark 6. Oil a baking tray. Turn out the dough and knead for 1 minute, until smooth. Gently roll out the dough to a round about 30 cm/12 inches in diameter – it doesn't have to be a perfect circle; a slightly oval shape is traditional.

4 Transfer to the prepared baking tray, cover with a clean tea towel or oiled clingfilm and leave to rise in a warm place for 20–30 minutes.

5 Make holes about 5 cm/2 inches apart all over the surface of the dough with the handle of a wooden spoon. Spread the onion rings over the dough, drizzle with the remaining oil and scatter over the salt.

6 Bake in the preheated oven for 20 minutes, then scatter over the rosemary sprigs and bake for a further 5 minutes, until well risen and golden brown. Transfer to a wire rack to cool slightly, then serve warm.

Caramelized Onion Tart

Serves 6–8

ingredients

- 100 g/3½ oz unsalted butter
- 600 g/1 lb 5 oz onions, thinly sliced
- 2 eggs
- 100 ml/3½ fl oz double cream
- 100 g/3½ oz Gruyère cheese, grated
- 20-cm/8-inch ready-baked pastry case
- 100 g/3½ oz Parmesan cheese, coarsely grated
- salt and pepper

1 Melt the butter in a heavy-based frying pan over a medium heat. Add the onions and cook, stirring frequently to avoid burning, for 30 minutes, or until browned and caramelized. Remove the onions from the pan and set aside.

2 Preheat the oven to 190°C/375°F/Gas Mark 5. Beat the eggs in a large bowl, stir in the cream and season to taste with salt and pepper. Add the Gruyère cheese and mix well. Stir in the cooked onions.

3 Pour the egg and onion mixture into the pastry case and sprinkle with the Parmesan cheese. Place on a baking tray and bake in the preheated oven for 15–20 minutes, until the filling has set and is beginning to brown.

4 Remove from the oven and leave to rest for at least 10 minutes. The tart can be served hot or left to cool to room temperature.

Onion Dhal

Serves 4

ingredients

- 100 g/3½ oz red split lentils (masoor dhal)
- 6 tbsp vegetable oil
- 1 small bunch of spring onions, chopped
- 1 tsp finely chopped fresh ginger
- 1 tsp crushed garlic
- 1½ tsp chilli powder
- 1½ tsp turmeric
- 300 ml/10 fl oz water
- 1 tsp salt
- 1 fresh green chilli, deseeded and finely chopped
- chopped fresh coriander leaves, to garnish

1 Rinse the lentils thoroughly and set aside until required.

2 Heat the oil in a heavy-based saucepan. Add the spring onions to the pan and fry over a medium heat, stirring frequently, until lightly browned.

3 Reduce the heat and add the ginger, garlic, chilli powder and turmeric. Briefly stir-fry the spring onions with the spices. Add the lentils and stir to blend.

4 Add the water to the lentil mixture, reduce the heat to low and cook for 20–25 minutes.

5 When the lentils are tender, add the salt and stir gently to mix well.

6 Transfer the onion dhal to a serving dish. Stir in the chilli and serve immediately, garnished with coriander.

Spring Onion, Pea & Ricotta Tartlets

Makes 12

ingredients

pastry
- 200 g/7 oz plain flour, plus extra for dusting
- pinch of salt
- 125 g/4½ oz butter, diced, plus extra for greasing
- 1 egg yolk

filling
- 250 g/9 oz ricotta cheese
- 100 g/3½ oz pecorino cheese
- 1 egg, beaten
- 12 spring onions, finely chopped
- 2 tbsp fresh shelled peas, lightly cooked and cooled
- 1 tsp green peppercorns in brine, drained
- salt and pepper

1 To make the pastry, sift the flour and salt together into a bowl, add the butter and rub in with your fingertips until the mixture resembles fine breadcrumbs. Add the egg yolk and enough cold water to form a smooth dough. Cover and chill in the refrigerator for 30 minutes.

2 Preheat the oven to 190°C/375°F/ Gas Mark 5. Lightly grease a deep 12-cup muffin tin.

3 Roll the pastry out on a floured work surface to a thickness of about 3 mm/⅛ inch. Using a pastry cutter, stamp out rounds large enough to line the cups of the muffin tin. Gently press the pastry cases into the cups. Line each pastry case with a small piece of baking paper and fill with baking beans.

4 Bake the pastry cases in the preheated oven for 4–5 minutes, until golden and crisp. Remove the paper and beans.

5 Meanwhile, to make the filling, mix the ricotta and pecorino cheeses together in a large bowl. Add the egg, spring onions and peas. Chop the peppercorns very finely, then add to the mixture. Season to taste with salt and pepper.

6 Spoon the filling into the pastry cases and bake for 10 minutes, or until golden. Serve warm.

Leek & Potato Soup

Serves 4

ingredients

- 25 g/1 oz butter
- 2 garlic cloves, chopped
- 3 large leeks, sliced
- 450 g/1 lb potatoes, cut into bite-sized chunks
- 2 tbsp chopped fresh parsley
- 1 tbsp chopped fresh oregano
- 1 bay leaf
- 850 ml/1½ pints vegetable stock
- 200 ml/7 fl oz single cream
- 100 g/3½ oz firm smoked cheese, grated
- salt and pepper
- snipped fresh chives, to garnish

1 Melt the butter in a large saucepan over a medium heat. Add the garlic and cook, stirring, for 1 minute. Add the leeks and cook, stirring, for 2 minutes. Add the potatoes, half the parsley, the oregano, bay leaf and stock, then season to taste with salt and pepper.

2 Bring to the boil, then reduce the heat, cover the saucepan and leave to simmer for 25 minutes. Remove from the heat, leave to cool for 10 minutes, then remove and discard the bay leaf.

3 Transfer half of the soup to a food processor and process until smooth (you may need to do this in batches). Return to the saucepan with the rest of the soup, stir in the cream and reheat gently. Adjust the seasoning, adding salt and pepper if needed.

4 Remove from the heat and stir in the cheese. Ladle into serving bowls. Garnish with the remaining parsley and the chives, and serve immediately.

Leeks with Yellow Bean Sauce

Serves 4

ingredients
- 450 g/1 lb leeks
- 175 g/6 oz baby corn
- 6 spring onions
- 3 tbsp groundnut oil
- 225 g/8 oz Chinese leaves, shredded
- 4 tbsp yellow bean sauce

1 Using a sharp knife, slice the leeks, halve the baby corn and cut the spring onions into 2.5-cm/1-inch lengths.

2 Heat a wok or frying pan, then add the oil and heat until it is smoking.

3 Add the leeks, Chinese leaves and baby corn to the wok. Stir-fry the vegetables over a high heat for about 5 minutes, or until the edges of the vegetables are slightly brown.

4 Add the spring onions to the wok, stirring to combine.

5 Stir in the yellow bean sauce. Continue to stir-fry the mixture in the wok for a further 2 minutes, or until the yellow bean sauce is heated through and the vegetables are thoroughly coated in the sauce.

6 Transfer the stir-fried vegetables and sauce to warmed serving dishes and serve immediately.

Chilled Garlic Soup

Serves 4–6

ingredients

- 500 g/1 lb 2 oz day-old country-style white bread, crusts removed, torn
- 5 large garlic cloves, halved
- 125 ml/4 fl oz extra virgin olive oil, plus extra for drizzling
- 4–5 tbsp sherry vinegar
- 300 g/10½ oz ground almonds
- 1.2 litres/2 pints water, chilled
- salt and white pepper
- seedless white grapes, halved to garnish

1 Put the bread in a bowl with just enough cold water to cover and leave to soak for 15 minutes. Squeeze the bread dry and transfer it to a food processor.

2 Add the garlic, oil, vinegar to taste, and the ground almonds to the food processor with 250 ml/9 fl oz of the water and process until blended.

3 With the motor running, slowly pour in the remaining water until a smooth soup forms. Taste and add extra vinegar if needed. Cover and chill for at least 4 hours.

4 To serve, stir well and adjust the seasoning, adding salt and white pepper if needed. Ladle into bowls, drizzle over a little oil and float grapes on top. Serve immediately.

Garlic Spaghetti

Serves 4

ingredients
- 125 ml/4 fl oz olive oil
- 3 garlic cloves, crushed
- 450 g/1 lb dried spaghetti
- 3 tbsp roughly chopped fresh parsley
- salt and pepper

1 Reserve 1 tablespoon of the oil and heat the remainder in a medium saucepan. Add the garlic and cook over a low heat, stirring constantly, until golden brown, then remove the pan from the heat. Do not allow the garlic to burn as this will taint its flavour.

2 Meanwhile, bring a large saucepan of lightly salted water to the boil. Add the spaghetti and the reserved oil, return to the boil and cook for 8–10 minutes, or until the spaghetti is tender but still firm to the bite. Drain thoroughly and return to the pan.

3 Add the oil and garlic mixture to the spaghetti and toss to coat thoroughly. Season to taste with pepper, add the parsley and toss well to coat again.

4 Transfer the spaghetti to a warmed serving dish and serve immediately.

Chapter 5
Pods & Seeds

Directory of Pods & Seeds

Pods and seeds are invaluable staples in the cook's kitchen, not least because many of them may be dried to increase their shelf life. They are also a useful source of vegetable protein.

Beansprouts

Packed with nutrients, these are the crisp, juicy shoots sprouted from mung beans. They are delicious raw in salads, or cooked in a stir-fry until barely wilted.

Broad beans

Broad beans have a unique flavour and are best lightly cooked if they are not to become mealy. Remove the outer skin after cooking if it is tough. They are delicious steamed and tossed with butter and lemon zest.

Butter and lima beans

Similar in flavour and appearance, these large, flat, cream-coloured beans have a floury texture when cooked. They are excellent with a garlicky tomato sauce as an accompaniment to roast lamb.

Cannellini and haricot beans

These small, ivory beans have a creamy texture when cooked. Both are delicious in salads, soups or stews, or puréed to make a nutritious alternative to mashed potato.

Chickpeas

Chickpeas resemble shelled hazelnuts and have a nutty flavour and a creamy texture. They are widely used in Indian and Middle Eastern cuisines.

Flageolet and borlotti beans

The pretty, pale green flageolet bean has a delicate flavour and soft texture, while the hearty borlotti bean is pinkish-brown with a sweetish flavour and firmer texture. It is often used in Italian bean and pasta soups.

Green beans

Both French beans and runner beans are delicately flavoured and benefit from steaming rather than boiling. Runner beans usually have to have their strings removed, but most French beans nowadays are stringless and simply need to be 'topped and tailed'. They are delicious simply anointed with butter, or served in salads.

Lentils

Brown lentils have a robust texture and flavour, and add substance to stews, stuffings and soups. Green lentils and Puy lentils are similar to the brown lentil, but have a slightly milder flavour. The tiny, dark grey-green Puy lentil is considered superior in flavour to other varieties. They are delicious in warm salads with a vinaigrette dressing and also make a hearty addition to stews. Red split lentils are ideal for thickening soups and stews, and are used to make the spicy Indian dish, dahl.

Peas

Fresh peas are incredibly versatile and can be cooked quickly, either by steaming or boiling. Dried split peas are interchangeable with red split lentils, although they need pre-soaking and take longer to cook. They are perfect for dahls, soups, casseroles and purées.

Red kidney beans

Kidney beans have a soft, mealy texture. They are essential for chilli con carne and Mexican refried beans.

Soya beans

Soya beans range in colour from creamy yellow to brownish-black. They are rich in protein and make a healthy addition to vegetarian dishes. They are used in a wide variety of foods including tofu, meat-replacement mince, soy sauce and miso paste. They are also an essential ingredient in Asian sauces, including black or yellow bean sauce, and hoisin sauce.

Sweetcorn

Sweetcorn is perfect plainly boiled and tossed with melted butter and sea salt. Unlike other vegetables, sweetcorn toughens if overcooked. Young ears need about 3 minutes in rapidly boiling unsalted water.

Chilled Pea Soup

Serves 3–4

ingredients
- 425 ml/15 fl oz vegetable stock or water
- 450 g/1 lb frozen peas
- 55 g/2 oz spring onions, finely chopped
- 300 ml/10 fl oz natural yogurt or single cream
- salt and pepper

to serve
- 1 tbsp extra virgin olive oil
- 2 tbsp chopped fresh mint
- 2 tbsp snipped fresh chives
- grated rind of ½ lemon

1 Bring the stock to the boil in a large saucepan over a medium heat. Reduce the heat, add the peas and spring onions and simmer for 5 minutes.

2 Leave to cool slightly, then strain twice, making sure that you remove any bits of skin. Pour into a large bowl, season to taste with salt and pepper and stir in the yogurt. Cover the bowl with clingfilm and chill in the refrigerator for several hours.

3 To serve, remove from the refrigerator, mix well and ladle into individual serving bowls. Drizzle with the oil and sprinkle with the mint, chives and lemon rind. Serve immediately.

Lemon Beans

Serves 4

ingredients

- 900 g/2 lb mixed green beans, such as shelled broad beans, French beans and runner beans
- 70 g/2½ oz butter or margarine
- 4 tsp plain flour
- 300 ml/10 fl oz vegetable stock
- 5 tbsp dry white wine
- 6 tbsp single cream
- 3 tbsp chopped fresh mixed herbs
- grated rind of 1 lemon
- 2 tbsp lemon juice
- salt and pepper
- strips of lemon zest, to garnish

1 Cook the beans in a saucepan of boiling salted water for 10 minutes, or until tender. Drain and place in a warmed serving dish.

2 Meanwhile, melt the butter in a saucepan. Add the flour and cook, stirring constantly, for 1 minute. Remove the pan from the heat and gradually stir in the stock and wine. Return the pan to the heat and bring to the boil, stirring.

3 Remove the pan from the heat once again and stir in the cream, herbs, and lemon rind and juice. Season to taste with salt and pepper. Pour the sauce over the beans, mixing well to coat thoroughly. Serve immediately, garnished with strips of lemon zest.

Spaghetti with Fresh Pea
Pesto & Broad Beans

Serves 4

ingredients
- 250 g/9 oz fresh shelled broad beans
- 500 g/1 lb 2 oz dried spaghetti
- salt and pepper

pea pesto
- 300 g/10½ oz fresh shelled peas
- 75 ml/2½ fl oz extra virgin olive oil
- 2 garlic cloves, crushed
- 100 g/3½ oz Parmesan cheese, grated, plus extra shavings to serve
- 100 g/3½ oz blanched almonds, chopped
- pinch of sugar
- salt and pepper

1 For the pesto, cook the peas in a saucepan of boiling water for 2–3 minutes, until just tender. Drain and transfer to a blender or food processor. Add the oil, garlic and Parmesan cheese and process to a coarse paste. Add the almonds and process again. Add the sugar and season to taste with salt and pepper. Set aside.

2 Blanch the broad beans in a saucepan of boiling salted water for 2–3 minutes, until just tender. Drain and leave to cool. Peel off the grey skins.

3 Bring a large saucepan of lightly salted water to the boil. Add the spaghetti, return to the boil and cook for 8–10 minutes, or until the spaghetti is tender but still firm to the bite.

4 Drain the spaghetti and return to the pan with the broad beans and pea pesto. Toss well and transfer to individual serving plates. Grind over a little pepper, top with the Parmesan shavings and serve immediately.

Potato & Split Pea Soup

Serves 4

ingredients
- 2 tbsp vegetable oil
- 450 g/1 lb floury potatoes, in their skins, diced
- 2 onions, diced
- 75 g/2¾ oz split green peas
- 1 litre/1¾ pints vegetable stock
- 60 g/2¼ oz Gruyère cheese, grated
- salt and pepper

croûtons
- 40 g/1½ oz butter
- 1 garlic clove, crushed
- 1 tbsp chopped fresh parsley
- 1 thick slice of white bread, diced

1 Heat the oil in a large saucepan. Add the potatoes and onions and cook over a medium heat, stirring constantly, for about 5 minutes.

2 Add the split green peas to the pan and stir together well.

3 Pour the stock into the pan and bring to the boil. Reduce the heat to low and simmer for about 35 minutes, until the potatoes are tender and the split peas are cooked.

4 Meanwhile, make the croûtons. Melt the butter in a frying pan. Add the garlic, parsley and bread and cook, turning frequently, for about 2 minutes, until golden all over.

5 Stir the cheese into the soup and season to taste with salt and pepper. Heat gently until the cheese is starting to melt.

6 Pour the soup into warmed soup bowls and sprinkle the croûtons on top. Serve immediately.

Broad Beans with Feta

Serves 4–6

ingredients

- 500 g/1 lb 2 oz shelled broad beans
- 4 tbsp extra virgin olive oil
- 1 tbsp lemon juice
- 1 tbsp finely chopped fresh dill, plus extra to garnish
- 55 g/2 oz feta cheese, diced
- salt and pepper

1 Bring a large saucepan of lightly salted water to the boil. Add the broad beans and cook for 2–3 minutes, until tender. Drain thoroughly and set aside.

2 When the beans are cool enough to handle, remove and discard the grey skins. Put the peeled beans in a serving bowl.

3 Combine the oil and lemon juice in a small bowl, then season to taste with salt and pepper. Pour the dressing over the warm beans, add the dill and stir gently. Adjust the seasoning, adding salt and pepper if needed.

4 If serving hot, add the cheese, toss gently and sprinkle with dill, then serve immediately. Alternatively, set aside the beans in their dressing to cool and then chill until required. To serve cold, remove from the refrigerator 10 minutes before serving to bring to room temperature. Taste and adjust the seasoning, adding salt and pepper if needed, then sprinkle with the cheese and dill.

Green Bean Salad with Feta

Serves 4

ingredients
- 350 g/12 oz green beans, trimmed
- 1 red onion, chopped
- 3–4 tbsp chopped fresh coriander
- 2 radishes, thinly sliced
- 75 g/2¾ oz feta cheese, crumbled
- 1 tsp chopped fresh oregano or ½ tsp dried oregano
- 2 tbsp red wine or fruit vinegar
- 5 tbsp extra virgin olive oil
- 3 ripe tomatoes, cut into wedges
- pepper

1 Pour about 5 cm/2 inches water into the base of a steamer or a medium saucepan and bring to the boil. Add the beans to the top of the steamer or place them in a metal colander set over the pan of water. Cover and steam for about 5 minutes, until just tender.

2 Transfer the beans to a bowl and add the onion, coriander, radishes and cheese.

3 Sprinkle the oregano over the salad, then season to taste with pepper. Whisk the vinegar and oil together and pour over the salad. Toss gently to mix well.

4 Transfer to a serving platter, add the tomato wedges and serve immediately or chill in the refrigerator until ready to serve.

Cheesy Sweetcorn Fritters

Makes 8–10

ingredients
- 1 egg
- 200 ml/7 fl oz milk
- 100 g/3½ oz plain flour
- ½ tsp baking powder
- 85 g/3 oz canned sweetcorn kernels, drained
- 4 tbsp grated Cheddar cheese
- 1 tsp snipped fresh chives
- 2 tsp sunflower oil

1 Put the egg and milk into a small bowl and beat with a fork.

2 Add the flour and baking powder and beat until smooth. Stir in the sweetcorn, cheese and chives.

3 Heat the oil in a non-stick frying pan over a medium heat. Drop in either teaspoonfuls or tablespoonfuls of the batter.

4 Cook for 1–2 minutes on each side, until the fritters are puffed up and golden. Drain on kitchen paper and serve.

Sweetcorn, Potato & Cheese Soup

Serves 6

ingredients

- 25 g/1 oz butter
- 2 shallots, finely chopped
- 225 g/8 oz potatoes, diced
- 4 tbsp plain flour
- 2 tbsp dry white wine
- 300 ml/10 fl oz milk
- 325 g/11½ oz canned sweetcorn kernels, drained
- 85 g/3 oz Gruyère, Emmenthal or Cheddar cheese, grated
- 8–10 fresh sage leaves, chopped, plus extra sprigs to garnish
- 425 ml/15 fl oz double cream

croûtons

- 2–3 slices of day-old white bread
- 2 tbsp olive oil

1 To make the croûtons, cut the crusts off the bread slices, then cut the remaining bread into 5-mm/¼-inch cubes. Heat the oil in a heavy-based frying pan and add the bread cubes. Cook, tossing and stirring constantly, until evenly coloured. Drain the croûtons thoroughly on kitchen paper and reserve.

2 Melt the butter in a large heavy-based saucepan. Add the shallots and cook over a low heat, stirring occasionally, for 5 minutes, or until softened. Add the potatoes and cook, stirring, for 2 minutes.

3 Sprinkle in the flour and cook, stirring, for 1 minute. Remove the saucepan from the heat and stir in the wine, then gradually stir in the milk. Return the saucepan to the heat and bring to the boil, stirring constantly, then reduce the heat and simmer.

4 Stir in the sweetcorn, cheese, chopped sage and cream and heat through gently until the cheese has just melted.

5 Ladle the soup into warmed bowls, scatter over the croûtons, garnish with sage sprigs and serve immediately.

Beansprout Salad

Serves 4

ingredients

- 350 g/12 oz fresh beansprouts
- 1 small cucumber
- 1 green pepper, deseeded and cut into matchsticks
- 1 carrot, cut into matchsticks
- 2 tomatoes, finely chopped
- 1 celery stick, cut into matchsticks
- 1 garlic clove, crushed
- dash of chilli sauce
- 2 tbsp light soy sauce
- 1 tsp wine vinegar
- 2 tsp sesame oil
- fresh chives, to garnish

1 Blanch the beansprouts in boiling water for 1 minute. Drain well and rinse under cold water. Drain thoroughly again.

2 Cut the cucumber in half lengthways. Scoop out the seeds with a teaspoon and discard. Cut the flesh into matchsticks and mix with the beansprouts, green pepper, carrot, tomatoes and celery.

3 Mix together the garlic, chilli sauce, soy sauce, vinegar and sesame oil. Pour the dressing over the vegetables, tossing well to coat. Spoon onto individual serving plates. Garnish with chives and serve.

Tuscan Beans on Ciabatta Toast with Fresh Herbs

Serves 2

ingredients
- 4 slices of ciabatta bread
- 1 tbsp olive oil
- 1 small onion, finely diced
- 1 garlic clove, crushed
- 250 g/9 oz canned butter beans, drained and rinsed
- 90 ml/3 fl oz water
- 1 tbsp tomato purée
- 1 tsp balsamic vinegar
- 1 tbsp chopped fresh parsley
- 1 tbsp torn fresh basil
- salt and pepper

1 Preheat the grill to medium. Place the ciabatta on a piece of aluminium foil on the rack in the grill pan. Grill until lightly browned, then turn and cook on the other side.

2 Meanwhile, heat the oil in a medium saucepan and cook the onion over a low heat, until soft. Add the garlic and cook for a further minute, then add the butter beans, water and tomato purée. Bring to the boil, stirring occasionally, and cook for 2 minutes.

3 Add the vinegar, parsley and basil and stir to combine. Season to taste with salt and pepper and serve over the slices of toasted ciabatta.

Hummus Toasts with Olives

Serves 4

ingredients
- 400 g/14 oz canned chickpeas
- juice of 1 large lemon
- 6 tbsp tahini
- 6 tsp olive oil
- 2 garlic cloves, crushed
- salt and pepper
- chopped fresh coriander and chopped stoned black olives, to garnish

toasts
- 1 ciabatta loaf, sliced
- 2 garlic cloves, crushed
- 1 tbsp chopped fresh coriander
- 4 tbsp olive oil

1 To make the hummus, first drain the chickpeas, reserving a little of the liquid. Put the chickpeas in a food processor and blend, gradually adding the reserved liquid and lemon juice. Blend well after each addition until smooth.

2 Stir in the tahini and 5 teaspoons of the oil. Add the garlic, season to taste with salt and pepper and blend again until smooth.

3 Spoon the hummus into a serving dish. Drizzle the remaining oil over the top and garnish with coriander and olives. Leave to chill in the refrigerator while preparing the toasts.

4 Preheat the grill. Place the slices of ciabatta on a grill rack in a single layer. Mix the garlic, coriander and oil together and drizzle over the bread slices. Cook under the preheated grill for 2–3 minutes, turning once, until golden brown. Serve hot with the hummus.

Falafel Burgers

Serves 4

ingredients

- 800 g/1 lb 12 oz canned chickpeas, drained and rinsed
- 1 small onion, chopped
- juice and rind of 1 lime
- 2 tsp ground coriander
- 2 tsp ground cumin
- 6 tbsp plain flour
- 4 tbsp olive oil
- watercress, to garnish
- tomato salsa, to serve

1 Put the chickpeas, onion, lime juice and rind and the spices into a food processor and process to a coarse paste.

2 Tip the mixture out onto a clean work surface or chopping board and shape into 4 patties.

3 Spread the flour out on a large flat plate and use to coat the patties.

4 Heat the oil in a large frying pan, add the patties and cook for 2 minutes on each side, until crisp. Garnish with watercress and serve with tomato salsa.

Mixed Bean & Vegetable Crumble

Serves 4

ingredients
- 1 large onion, chopped
- 125 g/4½ oz canned red kidney beans (drained weight)
- 125 g/4½ oz canned butter beans (drained weight)
- 125 g/4½ oz canned chickpeas (drained weight)
- 2 courgettes, roughly chopped
- 2 large carrots, roughly chopped
- 4 tomatoes, peeled and roughly chopped
- 2 celery sticks, chopped
- 300 ml/10 fl oz vegetable stock
- 2 tbsp tomato purée
- salt and pepper

crumble topping
- 85 g/3 oz wholemeal breadcrumbs
- 25 g/1 oz hazelnuts, very finely chopped
- 1 heaped tbsp chopped fresh parsley
- 115 g/4 oz Cheddar cheese, grated

1 Preheat the oven to 180°C/350°F/Gas Mark 4.

2 Put the onion, kidney beans, butter beans, chickpeas, courgettes, carrots, tomatoes and celery in a large ovenproof dish. Mix together the stock and tomato purée and pour over the vegetables. Season to taste with salt and pepper. Transfer to the preheated oven and bake for 15 minutes.

3 Meanwhile, to make the crumble topping, put the breadcrumbs in a large bowl, add the hazelnuts, parsley and cheese and mix together well.

4 Remove the vegetables from the oven and carefully sprinkle over the crumble topping. Do not press it down or it will sink into the vegetables and go mushy.

5 Return the crumble to the oven and bake for 30 minutes, or until the crumble topping is golden brown. Remove from the oven and serve hot.

Vegetable Chilli

Serves 4

ingredients

- 1 aubergine, peeled if wished, cut into 2.5-cm/1-inch slices
- 1 tbsp olive oil, plus extra for brushing
- 1 large red or yellow onion, finely chopped
- 2 red or yellow peppers, deseeded and finely chopped
- 3–4 garlic cloves, finely chopped or crushed
- 800 g/1 lb 12 oz canned chopped tomatoes
- 1 tbsp mild chilli powder, or to taste
- ½ tsp ground cumin
- ½ tsp dried oregano
- 2 small courgettes, quartered lengthways and sliced
- 400 g/14 oz canned kidney beans, drained and rinsed
- 450 ml/16 fl oz water
- 1 tbsp tomato purée
- salt and pepper
- chopped spring onions and grated Cheddar cheese, to serve

1 Brush the aubergine slices on one side with oil. Heat half the oil in a large heavy-based frying pan over a medium–high heat. Add the aubergine slices, oiled-side up, and cook for 5–6 minutes, until browned on one side. Turn the slices over, cook on the other side until browned and transfer to a plate. Cut into bite-sized pieces.

2 Heat the remaining oil in a large saucepan over a medium heat. Add the onion and peppers and cook, stirring occasionally, for 3–4 minutes, until the onion is just softened but not browned. Add the garlic and continue cooking for 2–3 minutes, or until the onion is just beginning to colour.

3 Add the tomatoes, chilli powder, cumin and oregano. Season to taste with salt and pepper. Bring just to the boil, reduce the heat, cover and simmer gently for 15 minutes.

4 Add the courgettes, aubergine and beans. Stir in the water and the tomato purée. Bring back to the boil, then cover the pan and continue simmering for about 45 minutes, or until the vegetables are tender. Taste and then adjust the seasoning, adding salt and pepper if needed. If you prefer a hotter dish, stir in a little more chilli powder.

5 Ladle into warmed bowls and top with spring onions and cheese.

Kidney Bean Risotto

Serves 4

ingredients

- 4 tbsp olive oil
- 1 onion, chopped
- 2 garlic cloves, finely chopped
- 175 g/6 oz brown rice
- 600 ml/1 pint vegetable stock
- 1 red pepper, deseeded and chopped
- 2 celery sticks, sliced
- 225 g/8 oz chestnut mushrooms, thinly sliced
- 425 g/15 oz canned red kidney beans, drained and rinsed
- 3 tbsp chopped fresh parsley, plus extra to garnish
- 55 g/2 oz cashew nuts
- salt and pepper

1 Heat half the oil in a large heavy-based saucepan. Add the onion and cook, stirring occasionally, for 5 minutes, or until soft. Add half the garlic and cook, stirring frequently, for 2 minutes, then add the rice and stir for 1 minute, or until the grains are thoroughly coated with the oil.

2 Add the stock and bring to the boil, stirring constantly. Reduce the heat, cover and simmer for 35–40 minutes, or until all the liquid has been absorbed.

3 Meanwhile, heat the remaining oil in a heavy-based frying pan. Add the red pepper and celery and cook, stirring frequently, for 5 minutes. Add the mushrooms and the remaining garlic and cook, stirring frequently, for 4–5 minutes.

4 Stir the rice into the frying pan. Add the beans, parsley and nuts. Season to taste with salt and pepper and cook, stirring constantly, until piping hot. Transfer to a warmed serving dish, sprinkle with parsley and serve.

Warm Red Lentil Salad
with Goat's Cheese

Serves 4

ingredients

- 2 tbsp olive oil
- 2 tsp cumin seeds
- 2 garlic cloves, crushed
- 2 tsp grated fresh ginger
- 300 g/10½ oz red split lentils
- 700 ml/1¼ pints vegetable stock
- 2 tbsp chopped fresh mint
- 2 tbsp chopped fresh coriander
- 2 red onions, thinly sliced
- 200 g/7 oz baby spinach leaves
- 1 tsp hazelnut oil
- 150 g/5½ oz soft goat's cheese
- 4 tbsp Greek yogurt
- pepper
- lemon wedges, to garnish
- toasted rye bread, to serve

1 Heat half the olive oil in a large saucepan over a medium heat, add the cumin seeds, garlic and ginger and cook, stirring constantly, for 2 minutes.

2 Stir in the lentils, then add the stock, a ladleful at a time, until it is all absorbed, stirring constantly – this will take about 20 minutes. Remove from the heat and stir in the herbs.

3 Meanwhile, heat the remaining olive oil in a frying pan over a medium heat, add the onions and cook, stirring frequently, for 10 minutes, or until soft and lightly browned.

4 Place the spinach in a bowl, pour over the hazelnut oil and toss well, then divide among individual serving plates.

5 Mash the goat's cheese with the yogurt in a small bowl and season to taste with pepper.

6 Divide the lentils among the plates and top with the onions and the goat's cheese mixture. Garnish with lemon wedges and serve with toasted rye bread.

Sweet Potato Curry
with Lentils

Serves 4

ingredients

- 1 tsp vegetable oil
- 100 g/3½ oz sweet potato, cut into bite-sized cubes
- 75 g/2¾ oz potato, cut into bite-sized cubes
- 1 small onion, finely chopped
- 1 small garlic clove, finely chopped
- 1 small fresh green chilli, deseeded and chopped
- ½ tsp ground ginger
- 50 g/1¾ oz green lentils
- 75–100 ml/2½–3½ fl oz hot vegetable stock
- ½ tsp garam masala
- 1 tbsp natural yogurt
- pepper

1 Heat the oil in a saucepan with a lid and sauté the sweet potato over a medium heat, turning occasionally, for 5 minutes.

2 Meanwhile, cook the potato in a saucepan of boiling water for 6 minutes, until almost cooked. Drain and set aside.

3 Remove the sweet potato from the pan with a slotted spoon, then add the onion to the pan. Cook, stirring occasionally, for 5 minutes, or until transparent. Add the garlic, chilli and ginger and stir for 1 minute.

4 Return the sweet potato to the pan with the boiled potato and the lentils, half the stock, the garam masala and pepper to taste. Stir well to combine, bring to a simmer and cover.

5 Reduce the heat and simmer for 20 minutes, adding a little stock if the curry looks too dry. Stir in the yogurt and serve.

Conversion Charts

temperatures

CELSIUS (°C)	GAS	FAHRENHEIT (°F)
110	¼	225
120	½	250
140	1	275
150	2	300
160	3	325
180	4	350
190	5	375
200	6	400
220	7	425
230	8	450
240	9	475

volume measures

METRIC	IMPERIAL
1.25 ML	¼ TSP
2.5 ML	½ TSP
5 ML	1 TSP
10 ML	2 TSP
15 ML	1 TBSP/3 TSP
30 ML	2 TBSP
45 ML	3 TBSP
60 ML	4 TBSP
75 ML	5 TBSP
90 ML	6 TBSP
15 ML	½ FL OZ
30 ML	1 FL OZ
50 ML	2 FL OZ
75 ML	2½ FL OZ
100 ML	3½ FL OZ
125 ML	4 FL OZ
150 ML	5 FL OZ
175 ML	6 FL OZ
200 ML	7 FL OZ
225 ML	8 FL OZ
250 ML	9 FL OZ
300 ML	10 FL OZ
350 ML	12 FL OZ
400 ML	14 FL OZ
425 ML	15 FL OZ
450 ML	16 FL OZ
500 ML	18 FL OZ
600 ML	1 PINT

weight measures

METRIC	IMPERIAL
5 G	⅛ OZ
10 G	¼ OZ
15 G	½ OZ
25/30 G	1 OZ
35 G	1¼ OZ
40 G	1½ OZ
50 G	1¾ OZ
55 G	2 OZ
60 G	2¼ OZ
70 G	2½ OZ
85 G	3 OZ
90 G	3¼ OZ
100 G	3½ OZ
115 G	4 OZ
125 G	4½ OZ
140 G	5 OZ
150 G	5½ OZ
175 G	6 OZ
200 G	7 OZ
225 G	8 OZ
250 G	9 OZ
275 G	9¾ OZ
280 G	10 OZ
300 G	10½ OZ
325 G	11½ OZ
350 G	12 OZ
375 G	13 OZ
400 G	14 OZ
425 G	15 OZ
450 G	1 LB
500 G	1 LB 2 OZ